Bae's Ballad

A Pocket Full of Crumbs

SECOND EDITION

RUTHA J. JONES

ISBN 979-8-89121-765-2 (softcover)
ISBN 979-8-89121-766-9 (hardcover)
ISBN 979-8-89121-770-6 (ebook)

Printed in the United States of America.

DEDICATION

To My Three Children
Billy, Linda and Timothy
and
My Fifteen Grandchildren
and
My Nineteen Great Grandchildren

ACKNOWLEDGEMENTS

I thank God for the wonderful and blessed life I have lived. I am thankful for my husband, Bill, for his support and inspiration to complete this book. I thank and acknowledge the family support from my sisters, Inez and Margie, and my children. Many thanks to my cousin, Dorothy White, who recreated a picture of the old farm house of our grandparents. I am so grateful for the special encouragement, organizational and clerical skills of Marian Diane Brown and Ella Sykes Harris.

—Rutha J. Jones

Although her writing _"A Pocket Full of Crumbs"_ was originally written for her children, grandchildren and great-grandchildren and friends, I would certainly commend it to her extended family and to others who might find a likeness of your own experiences within these pages.

It has been quite a struggle for Rutha to pick up the "bits and pieces" started almost 40 years ago and put them together, so remarkably. She had to depend on a power, a higher power; especially since dealing with serious health issues over the past 12 years, or so. She has encountered three strokes while dealing with chronic conditions: diabetes, high blood pressure and thyroiditis. Needless to say, she has encounter cognitive and physical impairment.

But yet, through it all with her determination, will power, fortitude, perseverance, and her dependence on Almighty God; she completed this work. If you know my wife, Rutha, this comes as no surprise to you, for she has always been led and driven by this Higher Power.

This is the same power that enabled her to be the virtuous wife and loving mother to our children. The same power that enabled her to do: the review, the recall, the research, and the revisits to old mentioned sites.

May she and her works continue to be as informative, uplifting and inspiring for you as they have been for me. I thank God for her and for the almost 69 years we have shared together.

Be blessed,
Bill Husband

Mom and Dad: We count ourselves truly blessed to have such "awesome" people in our lives. Yes, Dad, "AWESOME!!" You two are what makes our <u>race</u>, <u>state</u> and <u>country</u> a better place to be. With your endless love of God and family, that embodies you.

Love,
William and Jackie
Son and Daughter-in-law

To my wonderful mother: God dropped you off from Heaven to write, love and inspire your family. This book will help our family to learn the truth: There will be crumbs that may alter your life, hopefully

With Love,
Linda and James Paley
Daughter and Son-in-law

Congratulations, Mom!!!

Love,
Timothy Jones and Kids
Son

FROM THE AUTHOR'S DESK:

My book evolved from writings I did for my children as I approached my sixtieth birthday. I write of some of the people, places and experiences that shaped my life. I am a retired Registered Nurse who worked twenty-five (25) years in the Sexually Transmitted Disease Clinic, Memphis Shelby County Health Department. As supervisor, I directed and implemented a change in the image of the clinic setting and developed a non-judgmental approach to treatment and care. Many questioned how I became compassionate and understanding of the less fortunate and what some called *"low life"*. I am an advocate for the disenfranchised and dysfunctional.

My book depicts my life which is the story of many African-American women during the forties and fifties, living in the South when legal segregation was beginning to crumble, yet racial discrimination and limited opportunities were daily realities; living in the city with rural roots, nothing sensational, no acclaims to fame, but definitely a part of history.

Many people have touched me with sayings that became a part of the fabric of my life. Such a person was Uncle Cortrell, my paternal grandfather's youngest brother. He lived under the porch of Aunt Inez's house on Hemlock Street. He was a quiet, meek man, always with a smile. When asked, ***"How are you?"*** he always answered ***"No need to grumble when I have a pocket full of crumbs"***. He, who had seizures, was unable to work and lived in a dark, damp room, found no need to complain. He had a place to live and food to eat. I have tried to live with a positive attitude because of his saying which is the title of my book.

"I thank God for every remembrance of you" is one of my favorite scriptures. Prayer is a vital part of my life. I praise and glorify God with prayers of thanksgiving. He has been so good to me. I feel His Divine Intervention has been present in my life, guiding me to heights and places I could not imagine. These reflections revealed my *'pocket full of crumbs'*.

CONTENTS

Part 1
Living And Blessed
1933–1946

Part II
Living And Blessed
1947-1956

Part III
Living And Blessed
1957-1976

Joys And Sorrows
The Joys

Joys And Sorrows
Sorrows

WE CAME SEEKING

On a clear cloudless spring day, We journeyed via a
USA bus with Bob Jones driving us.
Many were asleep before we crossed the TN/AR Bridge.
We came seeking _____**REST**.
Skipping, limping and on a cane
To a mountain town, Eureka Springs.
We came seeking _____**KINDNESS**.
From Baptist, Church of God in Christ, Methodist,
Disciples of Christ, Nondenominational and Presbyterian
With names like Golden Leaf, Hill Chapel, Bloomfield,
Providence, Mt. Olive, Greater Imani, Mississippi Blvd.
And Parkway Gardens.
We came seeking _____**THE WORD**.
From north, east, south and west,
With hands uplifted and songs of praise.
Seeking spiritual growth through this worldly
maze, In our minds each one a queen.
We came seeking _____**JOY**.
From many paths and faith journeys abound
Mothers with daughters, sisters with sisters,
Co-workers with friends all around
We came seeking _____**FELLOWSHIP AND SISTERHOOD**.
Tired, overwrought and distraught
With grieving hearts for the loss of mother, sister,
Son, husband and friends. Sickness within us and all we hold dear.
We came seeking _____**STRENGTH AND PEACE OF MIND**,
As only God can give.
With joys for new births of grandchildren, birthdays
With high numbers, promotions, members of city council,
Boards and other heights of high esteem.
We came seeking _____**LOVE**.

Like flowers in Minnie's garden
All shapes, colors and heights
Tall, thin sisters and short, round sisters
We came seeking _____**INSPIRATION**.

"YOU CAN TELL THE WORLD"

Well you can tell the world about this
You can tell the nation about that
Tell'em what the master has done
Tell'em that the gospel has come
Tell'em that the victory's been won
He brought joy, joy, joy, joy, joy, joy, Into my Heart

Well my Lord spoke, He spoke so well
Yes He did, yes He did
Talked about the flames that burn in Hell
Yes He did, yes He did
Now my Lord spoke, He spoke so well
Yes He did, yes He did
Talked about the children of Israel
Yes He did, yes He did
He brought joy, joy, joy into my Heart

[Repeat 1st verse]

Well my Lord spoke, He spoke to me
Yes He did, yes He did
Talkin' about a man from Galilee
Yes He did, yes He did
My Lord spoke, He spoke to me
Yes He did, yes He did
Talkin' about a man from Galilee
Yes He did, yes He did
He brought joy joy, joy into my Heart

[Repeat 1st verse]

Well I don't know but I've been told
Yes He did, yes He did
Streets of Heaven are paved with gold
Yes He did, yes He did
Now the Jordan river is chilly and wide
Yes He did, yes He did
I got a home on the other side
Yes He did, yes He did
He brought joy, joy, joy into my Heart

TRAMPIN'

I'm trampin', trampin'
Tryin' to make Heaven my home I'm trampin', trampin'
Tryin' to make Heaven my home

I'm trampin', trampin'
Tryin' to make Heaven my home I'm trampin', trampin'
Tryin' to make Heaven my home

I've never been to Heaven
But I've been told
Tryin' to make Heaven my home

That the streets up there
Are paved with gold
Tryin' to make Heaven my home

I'm trampin', trampin'
Tryin' to make Heaven my home I'm trampin', trampin'
Tryin' to make Heaven my home

I'm trampin', trampin'
Tryin' to make the Heaven my home
Hallelujah, I'm trampin', trampin'
Tryin' to make Heaven my home

LORD, PLANT MY FEET ON HIGHER GROUND

I'm pressing on the upward way,
New Heights I'm gaining every day;
Still praying as I'm onward bound,
"Lord, plant my feet on higher ground."

Lord, lift me up and let me stand, by Faith,
on Heaven's tableland,
A Higher plane than I have found;
Lord, plant my feet on higher ground.

My Heart has no desire to stay
Where doubts arise and fears dismay;
Though some May dwell where those abound,
My prayer, my aim, is higher ground.

I want to live above the world,
Though Satan's darts at me are hurled;
For faith has caught the joyful sound,
The song of saints on higher ground.

I want to scale the utmost height
And catch a gleam of glory bright;
But still I'll pray till Heav'n I've found,
"Lord, plant my feet on higher ground."

BILL'S EXPERIENCES WITH DISCRIMINATION AND THE CIVIL RIGHTS MOVEMENT

I was asked to comment on experiences during the civil rights movement. I chose to interview Bill Jones. You have to understand the experiences that led up to the movement. Bill was born in 1929 during the great depression. As a nine year old walking on the sidewalk he met a white man and did not step off the pavement. Bill was tongue lashed! This was his first encounter with racism. As a teenager working at Halle on Main Street, he used the employee rest room. Although the door being unmarked, he was expected to know that this room was for *whites only*, by common knowledge. After serving in the U.S. Airforce as an officer; after completing his tour of duty and returning to Memphis in 1958, Bill called for information to enter the reserves and was told to come in to fill out the necessary paperwork. When he arrived, the clerk he had spoken to over the phone turned red. The clerk started stammering, many pauses, going in and out of the offices, calling others over the phone, and then finally he told Bill that there were no openings in his field, maybe in Little Rock, Arkansas.

These were just three of the many episodes in his life. So, he was ready to fight for change. The horrible murder of Emmett Till in Mississippi made many African Americans ready to fight or die for civil rights. In 1968, Bill took off from work (as a junior high school math teacher in the Shelby County school system) to be in the civil rights march for the city's sanitation workers.

The teachers had been advised by the principal to take a day of sick leave if they were to participate in the march. Bill refused. He wanted the record to show that he took the day off to join in the march. The marchers met at Clayborne Temple. Elders W.L. Jones and Dr. Vasco Smith with their church banners Parkway Gardens Presbyterian Church, U.S. were positioned over the front of the march. With Bill on one end and Dr. Vasco Smith on the other, it stretched the full width of Beale Street. As they turned from Beale Street north onto Main Street chaos broke out: showcase windows breaking, glass flying, people screaming—marshal (parade) yelling *"Turn back!! Turn back!!"* Police attacked the marchers with tear gas and clubs. They chased the marchers all the way back to Clayborne Temple where tear gas was farther used.

TO DREAM THE IMPOSSIBLE DREAM

To dream the impossible dream To fight the unbeatable foe
To bear with unbearable sorrow
To run where the brave dare not go
To right the unrightable wrong
To love pure and chaste from afar
To try when your arms are too weary
To reach the unreachable star
This is my quest to follow that star
No Matter how hopeless, no Matter how far
To fight for the right
Without question or pause
To be willing to march
Into Hell for a Heavenly cause
And I know if I'll only be true
To this glorious quest
That my Heart will lie peaceful and calm
When I'm laid to my rest
And the world will be better for this
That one man, scorned and covered with scars
Still strove with his last ounce of courage
To reach the unreachable star
The fight the unbeatable foe
To dream the impossible dream
And the world will be better for this
That one man, scorned and covered with scars
Still strove with his last ounce of courage
To reach the unreachable star
To fight the unbeatable foe
To dream the impossible dream.

JESU, JOY OF MAN'S DESIRING

Jesus, joy of man's desiring
Holy wisdom, love most bright
Drawn by thee, our souls aspiring
Soar to uncreated light

Word of God, our flesh that fashioned
With the fire of life impassioned
Striving still to truth unknown
Soaring, dying round thy throne Jesus, joy of man's desiring

Holy wisdom, love most bright
Drawn by thee, our souls aspiring
Soar to uncreated light

Word of God, our flesh that fashioned
With the fire of life impassioned
Striving still to truth unknown
Soaring, dying round thy throne

IF IT HAD NOT BEEN FOR THE LORD ON MY SIDE

If it had not been for the Lord on my side
Where would I be? Where would I be?
If it had not been for the Lord on my side
Where would I be? Where would I be?

He kept my enemies away
He let the sun shine through a cloudy day
Oh, He wrapped me in the cradle of his arms
When He knew I'd been battered and torn So…

[Back to chorus]

He never left me all alone
He gave me peace and joy I've never known
He answered when I knelt down to pray
And in victory, the Lord showed me the way

[Back to chorus]

THE JENKINS FAMILY OF DESOTO COUNTY

"You can tell the world about this! You can tell the world that I'm blessed!

The lines of this folk song/spiritual are sung by the Jenkins of Desoto County, Mississippi, for we are a blessed people. Many times I wondered where did certain characteristics come from and why are we this way? In search of the answers to these questions, a story developed. It begins with Samuel Jenkins. He was typical of many of his era, who did not talk about slavery. Little documentation is found of his life before 1870. So, with tidbits from family members, the story unfolds.

THE ROOT: A FIRM FOUNDATION

SamuelLaFayette Jones (1837-1915)
Mae LizaMartha Jones (1835-1921)

Good soil is necessary for a firm foundation. Soil is made up of broken bits of rock and mixed with the remains of living things. It is one of our most important resources. Jesus used the parable of good soil as an example of how to get a good crop. So it is with family. Our soil is a mixture of many types. When I visited Africa, I wondered if my ancestors were from Ghana, the beautiful land of the Ashanti people, there I was impressed with the former palace of kings and queens. Or maybe they were from the Ibo, the fierce and competitive people of Nigeria or the regal Masai herding their cattle in Kenya. Finally, I decided my ancestors were probably from Zaire. They were small dark friendly people. Most were not tall but walked upright and I was impressed with their warmth and hospitality. It was a feeling, nothing scientific, but I sensed a strong pull of kindred to the people. I saw no royalty; just ordinary people. So, the dark soil of the Congo mixed with white sand from England, and the reddish brown soil of Mississippi makes our foundation. Our people were farmers concerned with soil and dependent upon the land.

Our story begins with the birth of a slave, the grandmother of Samuel. We may never know the names of our African ancestors. They were brought to this country, suffered many hardships. They took a long journey across the Atlantic, packed in the hull of a ship. They experienced a change in climate and separation from tribal members, to name a few.

Roots collect water and food and sends up nourishment. Trees have a vast root system deep in the earth and provide an anchor to keep the tree upright. Our roots are grounded in the Eudora, Hacken Bottom area of Desoto County, Mississippi. Some of the land is now under water in the Arkubutla Dam. These roots give us an anchor through the floods and storms of life.

Sam Jenkins

SAM JENKINS (1855-1937)

Sam, my great grandfather, was born in 1855 in southern Mississippi. I was unable to find him in the census of 1870 in Mississippi. I wondered if Maybe He changed his name or came from a Louisiana plantation. Some of the big plantations of Warren County (Vicksburg) spilled over into Louisiana. I remember Aunt Inez mentioning Louisiana, but I can't remember the connection. I did find a Samuel Calvin Jenkins in the 1870 census living with messianic, presumably an eighty (80) year old grandmother in the Vicksburg area. He was the right age, fifteen; but was listed as deaf and dumb, unable to read or write. Sometimes he gave his parents birthplace as Alabama and at other times, the United States or unknown; or whatever he thought the questioner might want.

He was the last generation of slaves. He could be described as a tall black man with a crooked nose who lived with his family on the Ardmore plantation. His mother made many beautiful dresses for the ladies of the house. He played with the Ardmore children: Annie Elizabeth, Thomas and Henry. They played school where Annie Elizabeth taught him lessons her tutor had taught her. Sam listened well and soon was reading and writing. Henry teased him with knowledge he was sure Sam didn't know. Such as *"Sam doesn't know the earth is round"*. Sam marked these things as important and remembered them. He was unaware he talked like, had mannerisms, and a speech pattern of the Ardmores.

Mae Liza, his mother was a short, plump, dark skinned woman with typical Negroid features; thick lips, broad nose, and heavy hipped. She and her mother, a cook, came to Mississippi in the early 1800's. She was reared in and around the big house and had a sense of security although a slave. She sewed and helped in the kitchen. A quiet, stoic woman, who kept her anguish and frustration to herself when Samuel left; or as she thought, he was killed for his hot temper.

Sam's father, Samuel, it is thought, was brought to Mississippi in 1846 when more Negroes were needed to open up the lower southern states. He was considered temperamental or high strung and was sold frequently. He was a tall, dark man with a keen nose, thin lips and thick wooly hair. He was a loner, a man of few words, with a fiery temper who disappeared without revealing to Mae Liza or anyone, if it was planned.

When Sam was seven years old, his mother made him a uniform of red and black with yellow epaulets. He followed Uncle Joe the coachman and was allowed to drive the carriage to the main road. He loved horses and helped in the stables. His soft touch, quiet manner and talk had a calming effect on them. He traveled with the Ardmores to Natchez and New Orleans. He was inquisitive and learned to perform many tasks; shoe horses, cook, act as a valet and coachman. Rumors were ever present. Sam was ten years old when the slaves were freed.

In 1865, the Master told the slaves they were free. Mae Liza had lived through many changes; moving from North Carolina, different masters with different types of relationships to their slaves and now freedom. Warren County was one of the most heavily populated slave areas. After emancipation, Sam went to one of the schools started in the area by the Freedmen's Bureau. During the winter of 1869, Mae Liza died, after a short illness. Within six months, his grandmother and Uncle Joe died and his sister, Callie, moved with a family to northern Mississippi. With these relatives gone, Sam felt all alone and had thoughts of leaving Ardmore. He kept his thoughts to himself and daydreamed of finding Callie.

When told they were free, many slaves left the farms and plantations looking for *"freedom"*, jobs and family. Confusion was everywhere, fear of the unknown, and fear of the Yankees were prevalent. Many of the Yankees, sent to aid in the Reconstruction period were guilty of abusing, raping and pillaging. The only thing that helped to keep order and sanity among the ex-slaves was family, (biological or communal). The slaves developed relationships that made them a community. They called older people uncle and aunt, and when disaster came, or families were separated, a person from the community stepped up and became a surrogate parent to the children.

Many had never been off the plantations or away from the small towns and had no idea where they were going. Joining the exodus in 1874 was Sam Jenkins, looking for Callie Boyd, called Dorcas, in the Cub Lake area of northern Mississippi. My daddy always referred to Callie Boyd as Grampa Sam's sister. I was unable to verify this relationship and wonder if they were blood related for some of his grandchildren had not heard of her. It was whispered in the family that she followed a white man to north Mississippi. The tone used when saying this implied more than a servant/master relationship.

In 1874, Sam caught a ride to Memphis. He stayed in Memphis three months, working odd jobs and set out in August to find Callie. He bought a reddish brown horse and left on the Hernando Road. He heard they needed a teacher in the Hacken Bottom area. He was a reserved, quiet man with a different voice; knowledgeable of many things from his travels and formal education. He listened well and acted older than his nineteen years.

On the edge of a marsh, Sam rode up a slight incline and saw a small log cabin. The house was not as grand as the houses in southern Mississippi. This house had started with a dogtrot with one room on the east and a room and kitchen on the west. The dogtrot was later enclosed and used as a parlor. Two more rooms had been added. Sam stiffly dismounted, walked to the rear and inquired about a teaching job. The owner, Colonel Lute Jones, was a pharmacist. His father, a federal judge in Alabama, was granted four sections of land in Mississippi. On the father's death, the widow and her four sons moved to Mississippi. Each son was given a section (640 acres) of land. Some of the sons had added more land to their original and were wealthy landowners. Lute had no desire to own a great plantation. His interest was in the medicinal use of many plants and herbs used by the Native-Americans and slaves. He was known throughout the area as a great healer.

The land was low with slight elevations. Sam walked around, getting a feel of the area. He entered a meadow with lush green grass, tall oak and maple trees with Bob-o-links chirping. His heart was joyful, and He felt at home; and, though not considered a deeply religious man, He felt the presence of God. He was sure he would find Callie.

ELLA JONES JENKINS (1858-1924)

Sam Jenkins saw two girls sitting under a large oak tree. One looked like a white girl, big boned, pale skin, gray eyes, with dark brown hair and about fifteen or sixteen years old. The other was small boned, honey colored with full lips and about eight or nine years old. The one who looked white, looked Sam in the eyes and said, *"Who you?"* He was surprised—she had the voice of a Negro. Her name was Ella, and her sister's Janie. Janie had one leg shorter than the other. They were from a family of mulattoes…LaFayette or Fayette Jones, the father and Martha, the mother. The children were Ella, Reuben, LaFayette, Lizzie, Matt, Janie, Tommie and later, Carrie. They lived on land given to the father on the Lute Jones place. The relationship/kinship of LaFayette and Lute is unknown. Who were LaFayette's mother and father are questions unanswered. Was he one of the four brothers, disowned as he lived with a black woman?

Sam returned frequently to the grove where many gathered in the evenings. Ella, Janie and sometimes Lizzie were often there, sitting off to the side, under an oak tree. People of mixed blood many times felt ostracized. He entertained them with tales of his travels and jobs on the plantation. He explained why he came to the area, looking for his sister, Callie, in the Cub Lake area. How surprised he was to discover he was near the Cub Lake area. He soon located Callie and asked Ella to marry him.

Sam and Ella married in 1875, and lived with her family with their two children, LaFayette born in 1876 and Ida born February 12, 1880. Ida died of a childhood fever, at age seven. Ella could not read or write, but had *"mother wit"*. She was a deeply religious woman, who believed in the power of prayer. She was a no-nonsense, stern, business woman and farmer. They were members of the Pleasant Grove CME Church. After five years, she and Sam built a log cabin on her father's place. He taught and helped with the farm, but most of the work was done by Ella and the children, along with help from her brothers. Janie, Ella's sister helped with the children and later became a teacher. As was typical of most women of her time, Ella had children every year or two.

Sam was an immaculate dresser, articulate, a dreamer. He loved walking, reading and looking at sunsets. They liked to entertain and were well known in the community. Circuit preachers often had dinner at their home; and they traveled throughout the Delta and Northern Mississippi areas to church and community functions. Sam had many speaking engagements and Ella basked in his glory.

As a child, Sam had gone with his mother and grandmother to the Methodist church. They had to sit in the back of the church and listen to sermons by white ministers who stressed, *"Slaves, obey your masters!"* He stopped attending church as a youngster, but joined with Ella when the Colored Methodist Church was started in the area.

The Colored Methodist Episcopal Church was born after slavery in 1870 in Jackson, Tennessee. It was considered ultra conservative, striving for independence and self-sufficiency. Its members could exercise their own form of religious expression and participate in every phase of church life, including leadership and decision making. It shared with other black Methodists a firm commitment on the pursuit for social justice.

During Reconstruction, Negroes were able to vote and many were elected to the senate and congress. Negroes progressed in education, business, property ownership, self-assurance and efficiency. Many whites were frightened of the possibility of Negroes taking their jobs and them losing their position as superior beings. The Ku-Klux-Klan was organized and was used to terrorize, torture and lynch the former slaves.

The Jenkins' Family Home in Moore Town, Mississippi

THE TRUNK

The trunk with its thick wood offers solid protection from injury and provides and transports food. Some trees are evergreen, always the same, and others ornamental, colorful with beautiful flowers. All may act as windbreakers and are able to withstand many storms. Our trunk, the children of Sam and Ella, worked diligently to provide protection, support and financial security. They numbered nine.

1. **LaFayette** was born in 1876 in his parent's home. His wife's name was Melvina and their children were Lensie, Harvey, Tom, James, LaFayette, Freddie and Artrin.

2. **Ida** was born in 1880 and died in childhood. Many deaths occurred from infectious diseases.

3. **Rufus**, born 1883, my grandfather, and married Lula Ford. She was born in 1887. They had fourteen children: Cora, Dewitt, Rufus, Lula, A.D. (died in infancy), Irene, Earnest, Roxie, Clarence, Bertha, unnamed baby girl (buried in the garden), Lovey, Florida and Leroy.

Rufus was a stern, small boned man. He loved to hunt and fish and taught his sons the art of hunting and fishing. He made most of the furniture used in their home. Ownership of property was important to him because his father never owned any land. He brought his house in the Moore Town area in 1920. He worked the farm during the day and cut trees at night, sold timber, animal hides and vegetables. He rarely visited and never ate in anyone's home. He had a way with words, but used them sparingly. To him education was reading, writing and arithmetic, and when his children mastered these skills, he made them quit school. Each child was then given a plot of land, a cow and a pig. They became peddlers on the weekend: selling produce, turtles, rabbits, squirrels and skins. Rufus owned approximately 100 acres of land and rented more land from Lucious Nunnery.

Rufus and his family were members of Pleasant Hill Baptist Church. This church was built by his brother-in-law. He and his oldest son, Dewitt, were baptized together. The Masonic Lodge, a two-story building on the grounds was also used as a school. Grandpa Rufus thought our hope was in owning land and if you did, then you could control, to a large extent, how you lived.

His wife, **Lula**, my grandmother, was a quiet, brown skinned woman with high cheek bones (her mother was part Cherokee). She was very religious and known for her ardent prayers. She loved flowers and their yard had flowers of all descriptions. She was knowledgeable of folk medicine. The girls were taught sewing and needlework. They had garden plots and sold vegetables, eggs and needlework.

I remember the family sitting on the long front porch in the evening listening to stories, but surprisingly none on where the family came from. The importance was where we were going, we must "make it".

1. **Agnes**, born in 1888, had seizures. It is unknown whether her epilepsy was from birth, an injury or other causes. With all children delivered at home, many were born with birth defects. People with epilepsy were considered demon possessed. They were rarely taken from the home. It was considered a curse on the family. Ella and Sam were different as they carried Agnes to church and to visit relatives. Many times Agnes was tied to a chair to keep her from wandering off. She died from having a seizure and falling in an open fire,—while restrained.

2. **Sammie**, born in 1889, was a farmer. He and his wife, Jessie, had no children. He was known in the area as the speckled face man who rode a white horse. He had a skin disease. He had vitiligo which caused a loss of pigmentation with white patches, surrounded by normal skin. After his wife's death, with superstitious beliefs prevalent and no cure, he led a solitary life. This is the disease Michael Jackson is said to have and why he wears so much makeup, trying to mask his discoloration.

3. **Eugene**, born in 1893, was a farmer and peddler. He and his wife, Mattie, had two children: Tommie and Jonas. After farming for many years, he sold out and moved to

Memphis, where he sold vegetables. He brought two houses (one a duplex) on James Street, so he and his son could live side by side. I remember him with a wagon load of vegetables.

4. **Horace**, born in 1890 and married Estelle Bell. Her father owned a grist mill and many acres of land. It is rumored that Horace was killed in a fight over a woman. His wife and the Bell's took the children, Murry, called Buddy Bell and Mattie Ella. Mattie Ella was the first Jenkins to migrate north. In the seventy's, I visited her in Boston and was amazed at her resemblance to Aunt Inez.

5. **Cortrell** was born in 1897 and was never married. He had blackouts and lived with his sister Inez after his parent's death. He was a quiet, gentle man whose favorite expression was *"no need to grumble when I have a pocket full of crumbs"*. He loved to ride with my daddy, selling watermelons and fruits and other produce.

6. **Inez** was born in 1900 and was a school teacher in Mississippi. She was married to Hezekiah Glenn. She reared his daughter, Ruth, and their two children, Wilford and Joyce. In 1935, her salary was $35.00 a month. She was the first black woman in the area to own and drive a car. She and her father moved to Memphis in 1924, after Ella's death. Their home was a large white house on Hemlock Street. For many years she was the matriarch of the Jenkins family. She was a florist and a realtor; and, a strong advocate for education and self-help. She was socially active and a leader in Greenwood CME Church, and stressed to me *"you are from good stock"*.

She did talk of our heritage and made me aware of our roots. I regret I didn't listen as she talked of our lineage. Sometimes I thought her pretentious as she included our white kin. During the forties and fifties, I did not want to acknowledge this association. From her I learned I was not a country bumpkin, and could be proud of our rural background. I remember her collection of dolls lined up on the bed in her front bedroom. This was my first time seeing black dolls.

**1914 Photo: Rufus (Buster), Jr., Rufus Jenkins, Sr. holding
Lula, Lula holding Irene, Cora and Dewitt**

These ancestors lived during the times when blacks were considered less than a man. The purchase of property was made difficult. Many people were sharecroppers and the system was setup to sell the same things over and over. So, it was hard to pay for land or equipment. They were encouraged to buy from merchants on time and pay in the fall. Through hard work and perseverance they survived. It was difficult for them who had grown up playing with whites in a rural setting. They kept to themselves, worked hard and strived to make it.

BRANCHES

Branches make up the crown of a tree, a billowing cloud of witnesses. The leaves with their beautiful shapes get energy from the sun and make food for the tree to use. Our branches are the beautiful children of **LaFayette, Eugene, Horace, Rufus, Sr.** and **Inez**. Their children total more than twenty-three.

LaFayette (Melvina)

Lensie was born in 1889 and it was said he looked like **Grandpa Sam**. He was killed in a car wreck. The **LaFayette** name was passed down through his descendants: two children, **Mary and Fate. Harvey** was born in 1908 and he married a **Whitfield**. They had three children: **Eddie Lee, Earnestine** and **Harvey, Jr.** His wife died, and he later married **Beatrice**. She helped him to raise his three children.

Eugene (Mattie)

Tommie was born in 1913 and was married twice. He had no children. Jonas was born in 1917, and he and his second wife, Beatrice White had two children: **Reginald** and **Jonas, Jr.**

Horace (Estelle Bell)

Murry was called **Buddy**. When **Murry** was a child, his father was killed. He and his sister, **Mattie Ella**, and mother moved in with the maternal grandparents. He became known as **Buddy Bell** within the community. As an adult, he married "Pie" Toliver and they had four children. **Buddy Bell** died a young man; Pie and the children moved to New York. I can only remember the name of one child, Murline. **Mattie Ella** had three children and lived in Boston.

Rufus (Lula)

Cora was born in 1907 and never married. She assisted with the care of her mother's children and her brother's child, **Lovey**. She was the aunt who cared for me when I stayed with my grandparents during my parents' separations. She was very active in Pleasant Hill Baptist Church, and kept her membership there when she moved to Memphis after her parents' death. She was active in Sunday school where she never missed a Sunday for fifty years. She sold needlework, eggs, and vegetables from her garden, and it is said, she even sold ice water.

Dewitt was born in 1908, and was a farmer and government worker. He had one child, **LaFayette**, who was called **Fate**. He was married to Clara Burnette. Uncle Dewitt, Aunt Clara and Fate lived with us for a while on Hemlock Street. Fate looked a lot like my Daddy and was four years older then I. Fate was smart and the teachers thought I would be smart also. They stayed in Memphis about three years before moving to Hernando. He farmed many acres and owned big farm equipment, tractors, combines and cotton pickers. He contracted out to other farmers. Later he held the position of Supervisor of Roads with the county government. He was a Deacon at Pleasant Hill and Second Baptist churches. I liked to visit them and eat good tea cakes.

Rufus, Jr. was born in 1910. He was my father and his nickname was Buster. He was an entrepreneur, small business operator, trucker, tailor, carpenter, and performed many more jobs. He was married to Mattie Robinson. They had two children, Rutha and Inez. His second wife was Mary Jones. He was the first to leave the farm and had many jobs. He worked for the WPA in Mississippi for a year and about three months at a bakery in Memphis. He had a problem working for others and started making jobs—whatever and wherever needed. No job was too little or too big for him, as he was a *"jack of all trades"*. He was a stern, no nonsense taskmaster, demanding commitment from each person. He was a great singer, knowledgeable of the Bible, a great story teller and mimic. He was a rebellious, sometimes recluse person and a strong advocate for justice. He did not allow white men to come to the house, but would meet them on the corner or on the square. He always referred to himself as Jenkins so people could not call him by his first name. He loved hunting and gardening. He served in the Armed Forces, WWII, and was discharged with a disability, probably from his rebellious nature. His house was always open for his brothers and sisters as their *"Home"* in Memphis. His daughters, Rutha and Inez, were not allowed to work in the homes of whites as a means of protecting them from white men.

Lula was born in 1912. She married Sol Miller and was a peddler and farmer, where she sold eggs, vegetable and needlework. She and Sol had one child, A. D. Miller, who died in infancy. Lula's nickname was "Sis A" or "Sister Baby". She later married A.B. Balfour and returned to the farm after this marriage failed. She was very independent and made a good living selling crocheted items and her needlework. She helped Cora with providing childcare for her nieces and nephews. She was friendly and outgoing. Lula was the sister closest to my mother, who showed her love, concern and compassion. When mother was called on to pray at a church meeting, she told mother to kneel and she began to pray. She kept a warm relationship with mother after the divorce. She was an active member of Pleasant Hill Baptist Church in Moore Town.

Irene was born in 1913. She was a homemaker, farmer and day care teacher. As was common with the girls during that time, she married into a prosperous rural family. She married Charlie Dockery and had eight children: Willie Roy, Elroy, Detroit, Charles, Lorene, Rufus, Bobbie and Christine. I can remember when I was a child there was always news of a new baby being born in the family. I would see them mostly at funerals or our grandparents' home. My father and his siblings visited the farm house most Sundays. Irene was my quiet, reserved aunt, who took no nonsense, but was always smiling with a sparkle in her eyes. She was active in Pleasant Grove CME Church, as a missionary, stewardess, choir member and the Church secretary. She and Charlie were married for forty-two (42) years before his death. Irene taught for twenty-five (25) years at Northwest Head Start Center.

Earnest was born in 1916. He was a farmer and a Health Care worker for the Veterans Hospital. He married Ruth Hightower. They had one son, Earnest, who was called *"Boyce Lee"*. He later married Lovelle Fouse, and to that union, two children were born: Earnestine and Sandra. Earnest was an uncle who stayed with us as a young man. In our family, the children were paired with an older child. My Daddy was responsible for Earnest, therefore Earnest was like my big brother. He combed our hair, baby sat and reprimanded us as needed. He had a beautiful cafe au lait complexion, black curly hair and was considered a ladies man. He was adventurous, a sharp dresser and he loved pretty cars. Some of his cars were used in the Black yearly Cotton Makers Jubilee parade. His cars were usually white convertibles with a red stripe; and he would dress in the same colors. From listening to Charlie Parker and Louis Jordan with him, I developed a love of rhythm and blues and jazz music. Earnest loved sweets, especially ice cream. I can remember eating biscuits and homemade jam at his home. He rarely ate meat. He loved gardening and kept the community and church members supplied with his fresh vegetables. His son, Boyce Lee was the first baby I remember holding. Earnest was a paratrooper in WW!! He was wounded in action. He was a member of East Trigg Baptist Church.

Roxie was born in 1918. She was a homemaker, seamstress and hat maker. She was married to Tommie White and had twelve children: J.T., Rufus Lee, Ananias, Sammie, Roxie Mae, Gloria, Dorothy, Juanita, Roy Lee, Larry, Tyrone and Cynthia. Roxie is the aunt who was outgoing, full of energy with pretty sparkling eyes. Her house was always full of children and laughter. I remember her vibrant colored clothes, fancy hats and the fun her children had with each other. How I wished I had had many sisters and brothers. I remember when three or four family members lived on the farm. I loved going from house to house eating and especially at Roxie's house eating *"butter rolls"*, a fat-filled country dish. I had my first experience with a hospital when she delivered Roxie Mae. She was very independent, and continued to live in her house alone after her husband's death; and, after going blind in her early seventies. She would stress the importance of our family's need to have examinations for diabetes, heart trouble and cancer, which were the common causes of our ancestor's deaths. Roxie was an evangelist and a member of Mt. Vernon Baptist Church.

Clarence was born in 1921 and he was a shoe repairman, a tailor and a photographer. He especially loved working with leather. He was married to Ophelia Fitzgerald. There were no children born in this union. He later married Marion Carnes and fathered six children. They were: Clarence, Jr., Larry, Rachelle, Daryl, Randy and Angela. Clarence was another uncle I considered a brother. He lived with us on Hemlock Street, even married at our house. He was handsome, a sharp dresser with a distinct speech pattern that we called *"proper"*. Clarence served in the U.S. Armed Forces in World War II. He was a hard worker, with a hot temper. I remember my fear and anguish when he as a young man got in trouble with the law. In 1954 he moved to Milwaukee and became a successful business man. When he retired he spent his time gardening.

Bertha was born in 1923, and was a home maker who loved quilting and farming. She married Eddie Bachus and they had 8 (eight) children. They were Eddie Lee, Earnestine, Margaret, Linda, Edward Earl, Tommie, Bertha and Christine. The baby girl, Bertha, who looks like Aunt Inez, was the family historian. She has a quilt with the names listing three generations. Bertha had great courage and sent her young daughters, Eddie Lee and Earnestine, away to Mississippi School for the Deaf. She had been married for fifty years. I often think of her singing and her gift of making quilts. Bertha was very artistic and started painting after the age of sixty, when arthritis made it difficult for her to quilt or do needlework. She created beautiful quilts that were displayed at the Museum of Southern Folklore in Memphis. Bertha was a quiet, even tempered religious woman, an active member of Rising Sun Baptist Church. She was on the Mother's Board, sang in the choir and a Sunday school teacher.

Lovey was born in 1925 and became a factory worker. He married Azalee Williams and had three children: Lovey, Jr., Jerry and Elizabeth. Elizabeth was reared by her aunts, Cora and Lula. Lovey looked and acted a lot like Grandpa Rufus: quiet, a man of few words with a refined air. He sang in the choir of Mount Gilliam Baptist Church. His joys were singing and working in the yard. I can remember Lovey rushing in from the fields, twelve o'clock, to hear Sonny Boy Williams. This gave me a love for the Delta or **"Down Home"** blues.

Florida also known as **Floyd**, was born in 1928. He was a farmer, factory worker and deputy sheriff. He married Hattie Lomax and twelve children were born from their union. Their children were Carolyn, Anthony, Florida Jr., Ricky, Kathy, Linda, Danny, Delores, Melba, Marsha, Tracey, and Terry. Floyd was another uncle who was like a brother to me. He stayed with us on Hemlock Street. I remember when he tried to teach me to ride a horse, and when I walked with him on dusty roads searching for plums. He was a compassionate person and was concerned with all activities of our family members. Floyd was the brother who remained in the area and lived on part of the old place, in a beautiful house built by his sons. He was well-known in the community and many relatives and friends would visit to hunt and fish. He served as a deacon at Pleasant Hill Baptist Church.

Leroy was born in 1931 and worked in a factory. He was a small business operator. He was married to Thelma Hightower. They had eight children together: Larry, Leroy, Jr., Diane, Sharon, Deborah, Phyllis, Kerry and Karlos. Leroy was the *"baby"* of the family, with all the love that carries. We vied for Mama Lula's and Cora's attention. I remember us playing under the big oak tree with spools and animals whittled by his father and older brothers. He was a great artist and at an early age could draw animals and activities seen on the farm. I always wondered why I didn't have his talent. Leroy was a people person, he was a charmer.

He worked for years in a factory then went into business for himself. He was a member of Middle Baptist Church in Whitehaven.

<u>Inez</u> is the mother of Wilford Glenn and Gwendolyn Joyce Vinson. Wilford Glenn, was a musician and a music teacher. He was married to June Renee. Wilford was the first in the family to get a college degree. He taught in the Shelby County school system for thirty years. He attended the Chicago Conservatory and graduated from the University of Arkansas. He helped many boys and girls develop by participating in a choral group. He was a church musician for many years at Greenwood CME where he grew up and Mt. Olive CME where he was a member. He managed his mother's properties and became astute in business.

He loved gardening and supplied his friends and relatives with vegetables. I developed a love of classical music listening to Wilford practice on the piano. We sneaked and listened to his father's extensive Blues collection, which included a large collection of Bessie Smith. He loved to play tennis, had a large court in his yard. He also collected toy trains from childhood. He and June had four children: Wilford Jr. who was a Pastor with COGIC in Houston, Texas and is currently a music teacher; Stephen (deceased); Stephanie, a musician and a Shelby County (Memphis) school teacher who is married with one (1) son; and, Latissia, is a musician at Friendship Baptist Church and she has one (1) daughter.

Gwendolyn Joyce Vinson is a school teacher. She married Earl Vinson who is a college administrator. They have three children. Joyce is quiet, sophisticated, and always has the poise and dignity expected of a young lady. I always think of her as one of Aunt Inez's beautiful black dolls. Joyce worked in many places as a school teacher. She and her husband now live in the Seattle, Washington area.

LEAVES

The tree now towers high above ground. It never stops growing with seeds and buds. It gives shade and withstands the long cold winters and hot humid summers. The children listed below (greatgrandchildren of Sam and Ella) have reached many heights. The first medical doctor in the family was Margaret Ann Bachus. The first to earn a PhD is Earnestine Jenkins. Our family's first TV celebrity and author was Mary Jenkins Langston, Elvis Presley's cook. Among the numbered are preachers, teachers, nurses, social workers, engineers, computer specialists, business owners and artists. We are active in the church and our communities; and, we number eighty-nine. We, too, are hard workers with great perseverance and the ability to succeed. Many are the children of the forties, fifties, and sixties, who were part of the Civil Rights Movement. We marched, sat-in lunch counters, integrated schools, libraries and stores. Some of us were the first blacks in positions in places of employment. The climate was never perfect, some of us slipped in the floods, but strong arms pulled us back to safety.

The leaves are the **grandchildren** of:

Lensie

Mary was the cook for the famed Rock n Roll performer, Elvis Presley, a TV celebrity and a book author.

LaFayette, Jr. (Fate) is the father of 3 (three) children.

Harvey

Earnestine moved to Chicago and as a teenager; **Eddie Lee** has 2 (two) children **Harvey Jr.** I could not locate him.

Eugene

Tommie married twice and has no children;

Jonas has 2 (two) children: **Jonas, Jr. and Reginald.**

Jonas, Jr. is the father of 2 (two) children

Reginald is a realtor with 3 (three) children

Horace

He was killed in a fight; his wife and her parents raised their 2 (two) children):

Murry was called **Buddy Bell** and moved to New York after W WII had 5 (five) children, but I can only remember one of their names, **Merline**.

Mattie Ella moved to the Boston area in the 1930's. She is the mother of 3 (three) children.

Rufus Jr.

He was called Buster and married Mattie Robinson. They had 2 (two) children: **Rutha and Inez.**

Rutha is a registered nurse and writer. She and her husband, Willie Lee (Bill) Jones, have three children:

William A. Jones, an insurance broker and Pastor of a United Methodist Church. He and his wife, Jackie are the parents of 1 (one) child.

> **Alexis**

Linda Joy Paley {James} is the co-pastor with her husband at Spirit of Deliverance Center. She has (3) three children:

> **Gregory Theodore Walter** is the father of 2 (two) children.
>
> **Isaiah Walter**
>
> **Justin Walter** has 1 (one) child

Timothy Lloyd Jones is a warehouse worker and the father of 11 (eleven) children:

> **Timothy Jr., Terrell, Aaron, Pebbles, Catarra, Zuri, Zion, Ivory, Je'Kory, Marquezz and Timberly**

Inez Jenkins Payne became a practical nurse, business owner and a travel agent. She and her husband (Emmet Jr) have three children:

Michael Payne is deceased and fathered 2 children:

> **Michael Jr.,** is the father of 1 (one) child.
>
> **Demetria** is a registered nurse and mother of 3 (three) children.

Kenneth Payne

David Payne is the father of one child:

> **Ebonee**

Lula:

Her child died in infancy.

Irene: She was the mother of 8 (eight) children:

> **Willroy** became a business man and farmer. He was the father of 5 (five) children:
>
> > **Diane, Sharon, Debralynn, Dennis and Willroy, Jr.**
>
> **Elroy** carried on the family tradition of farming and owned a sausage factory. He is the father of 4 (four) children.
>
> > **Sharon, Diane, Meneral, Elroy Jr. all great singers.**
>
> **Detroit** is deceased and the father of 1 (one) child.
>
> > **Troy**
>
> **Charles** is a school teacher. He is the father of 2 (two children):
>
> > **Andrea**
> >
> > **Jason**
>
> **Lurine** became an elementary school principal. She was the mother of 2 (two) children:
>
> > **Pamela**
> >
> > **Melissa**
>
> **Rufus** is a business/trucking company owner. He is the father of two children:
>
> > Kim
> >
> > Kirby
>
> **Bobbie** is the mother of 1 (one) child:
>
> > Zondra.
>
> **Christine**

Earnest was the father of 3 (children):

> **Earnest, Jr. (Boicy Lee)**
>
> **Earnestine** received her Ph. D. and is a college professor.
>
> **Sandra** is an elementary school teacher.

Roxie was an evangelist, a hat maker and the mother of 12 (twelve) children:

J.T. died in a house fire.

Rufus Lee was killed in car wreck.

Sammie died in infancy.

Ananias has three children. I only remember one name.

Brenda

Roxie Mae was an office manager and the mother of 2 (two) children.

Damien is an engineer.

Jyrell is a music producer.

Gloria was the mother of two children:

Marc

Jerell

Dorothy is an artist and a school teacher.

Juanita is a fashion designer and an airline stewardess. She is mother to 1 (one child):

Venezia

Venezia has one child, **Addison**

Roy Lee is an apartment manager and father of 4 four children:

Reginald, Shana, Michael and Clarice.

Larry is a business owner and painter, with 2 (two) children:

Shante and B.J.

Tyrone is a business owner and a brick mason, and 2 (two) children:

Tynesha and Tyra.

Cynthia is a beauty salon owner with 1 (one) child,

Marchallo.

Clarence was the father of 5 (five) children:

Clarence, Jr.

Larry has (3) three children.

Rachelle is the mother of three children:

Shanne, Daryl and I cannot remember the 3rd child.

Randy is the father of two children.

Angela is a registered nurse.

Bertha was the mother of 8 (eight) children:

    Eddie Lee is a government worker.

    Earnestine is deceased and she had 1 (one child).

    Margaret Ann is a medical doctor, business owner and farmer. She has 2 (two) children:

    Bobby Valentino is an international musician

      Arletha

    Linda is a radio personality, "MAPCO Lady" and has two children.

    Edward Earl

    Tory

    Bertha is the mother of 3 (three) children.

    Christine is a social worker with 2 (two) children.

Lovey is the father of 3 (three) children:

    Lovey, Jr.

    Jerry

    Elizabeth is the mother of 5 (five) children.

Florida was a factory worker, sheriff's deputy and farmer, with 11 (eleven) children:

    Carolyn

    Anthony is a teacher and athletic director at the Desoto School System. He has two children:

      Camille

      Antoinette

    Florida, Jr., is a carpenter. He and his brother, **Danny**, built a house for their parents. He is the father of 2 (two) children:

      Brandon and Kyle.

    Ricky was killed in car wreck.

    Kathy is a school teacher with 1 (one) child:

John Jackson

Linda is a registered nurse and mother of 1 (one) child:

Courtney.

Danny (Bill) is a school teacher and carpenter. He helped to build a house for their parents. He is the father of 3 (three) children:

Raven, Olivia and Daniel.

Delores is the mother of 3 (three) children:

Sidney Evans, III and Bryan. Melba cares for her sister, **Carolyn Marsha** has three children:

Christopher, Ricky and Clarett.

Tracy has 2 (two) children:

Syria and Sebastian Dyer

Leroy is the father of 8 children:

Larry is a government worker and has 2 (two) children:

Shannon and **Nakesha**

Leroy, Jr. is an artist with two children,

Tiffany and Erin

Diane is an interior decorator and business owner, with two children:

Deshanne and Daryle

Sharon is a social worker and has one child:

Wendi

Deborah has one child:

Malcom

Phyliss

Kerry has one child:

Jessica

Karlos is a business owner with a barber shop. He has one child:

Kamiah

THE CROWN

The **tree** continues to grow with flowers and twigs all around it. Though old and bent, the young twigs continued to obtain strength, support and nurturing from the legacy of Sam Jenkins and they continue to pass it on.

These children, the great-grandchildren continue to pass on the legacy of Sam, with much determination, perseverance, and an inquisitive nature, the ability to learn from experience as well as education, artistic, love of beauty, family oriented and self-assurance. And from Ella, strong religious conviction, strong work ethic, stern reserved business manner and an assertive, independent life style. They number in the hundreds.

"You can tell the world about this. You can tell the nation we're blessed.
And it brings joy, joy, joy to our souls".

BUSTER

"DANCE TO YOUR OWN MUSIC"

Buster was born on January 21, 1910 in Desoto County, Mississippi and was the third of fourteen children. He is fair-skinned with tightly curled reddish brown hair, five feet and eleven inches, but appeared taller. He has broad shoulders, muscular arms and large hands. He has soft brown eyes which are ever alert, with good peripheral vision. At the age of 8 (eight) he was responsible for his brother Earnest. His demeanor is pleasant but business like, he states he has worked all of his life and feels that everyone else should do the same.

His father was a stern, hardworking man, typical of many of his generation, who showed very little emotion and no expression of love. The love Buster received was from his mother and sisters. He received more attention from his mother as he was sick with a fever for over a year. He became a manipulator, especially of his mother and sisters. With his brothers he was antagonistic, threatening and demanding. Fighting was his method of solving problems. His father rarely attended church but the mother took them every meeting Sunday. They sang as a quartet or group.

At age eighteen, Buster was "read out" of the church when a young girl named him the father of her child. He denied the allegation and would not repent. He became bitter and delighted in telling of the hypocrisy of the minister and members. In 1928, he and his friend Zelmo decided to go north looking for better jobs and the freedom that supposedly existed there. They left in Buster's 1929 Ford and traveled to St. Louis, Chicago and Milwaukee. Zelmo was called to preach and Buster was a good singer and prayed long and loudly, so they made a good team. The city dwellers were longing for down home preaching and services. They became homesick and returned home with the first snow fall. Zelmo returned later to Milwaukee and became a renowned Baptist minister.

In 1931, Buster married Mattie Robinson. He worked as a farmer, laborer and bootlegged whiskey. They had two daughters and moved to Memphis. He continued his zest to make it as a peddler and transporting farm labor. He was a stern disciplinarian, everything revolved around him. His wife and children anxiously awaited his arrival to determine his mood.

At times he was gregarious, a great story teller and mimic. For many years he visited a small sundry store, on Highway 51 now Elvis Presley where he and his friends drank coffee and told stories about their hunting dogs, women, politics and religion. He was generous to his family members. He gave fruits and vegetables to customers who were having a hard time and rarely loaned money as he says, *"This only makes enemies."* For many years sewing was his Sunday job, now he cooks and sews daily. He was very conservative with money and believed you only need one outfit per season. Buster is now eighty-three and lives alone. Buster knows he is difficult and said he didn't need anyone, but now is lonely. He decides to move back to Hernando, build a house on three acres and sells produce near the railroad crossing of Commerce Road. He walks slowly, still has a strong singing voice, firm handshake and determined to be his own boss.

I called my father, Daddy
From my earlies remembrances He was the rock—though odd.
He lovingly made me a baby bed
For his first born
That was his nature
Make what you need
His name was Rufus, Jr., He was called "Buster"

He was a rare, rebellious man, who danced to his own music. He was unusual and eccentric. He did things his way. A fair man, who focused on his duty, concerned with work. Buster was unlettered and unique in his ideals and personality, yet sincere and skillful. He was a man who boasted about his daughter, yours truly, whom he called, *"beautiful and smart"*. He was unlike others in expressing his love of God and man. He was like a towering oak tree with deep roots.

From my father I developed a strong work ethic, *"for you must work for what you want and it's not necessary to be like everyone else"*. I can hear daddy saying, *"Live so you don't have to say, 'I could have been, or I could have done'."* As I walked, I wondered what difference have I made? Did the things I have done matter? Many times I feel like an 'outsider'. Why? I Hear daddy saying, *"An empty wagon makes a lot of noise; don't lend money, it will cause lost friendship and don't get too high, so you don't have too far to fall."*

Growing up with my verbally abusive father, I experienced fear. Daddy only threaten to whip me once, and that was for losing or misplacing a new pair of shoes. What Daddy said was the law and he was always right. Mother was a buffer in our house. She could get Daddy to calm down, or see things in a different way. Mother told us stories or recited poems, sang songs and made our home pleasant.

My father was an outcast from his family, but they showered him with love. He didn't attend church, always wore work clothes and rebelled against *"Jim Crow or the southern system*". He owned land, his house, car and trucks and considered a good provider. He didn't believe in frills or niceties, and also considered himself a rough, ordinary man. He was a great storyteller, could be funny. He told stories of his experiences in life, made them funny and how he was not afraid and didn't need anyone.

TRAMPIN'

I'm trampin', trampin'
Try in' to make Heaven my home"

THE REDDING AND ANN STAPLE ROBINSON FAMILIES OF DESOTO COUNTY

Redding and his brother's last names were Stevenson before they were sold to the Robertson plantation. Redding's brother ran off and changed his name to Handy, and settled near Mount Bayou, Mississippi.

The children of **Redding and Ann Staple Robinson** were:

Joe Si (Anne): There were no children born of this union.

Luke (Lucy): They were the parents of 2 (two) children.

Alf (Ida): They were the parents of 8 (eight) children.

Dave: He never married. He was a cripple, and a musician. He played the harp.

Paul (Rosie):

Liza (Jim Self): He was a farmer, and had five children. He was a large land owner.

Margaret: They were the parents of nine children.

Rosie: She was called "Hon". She never married.

Matilda (Jonas Love): Her nickname was "Dank". She never married.

Mattie: She was called "Til". She had no children.

She had no children and never married.

ALFRED ROBINSON: A CHILD OF THE KING

Many groups research their family tree and find Kings and Queens among their ancestors. They stress their importance through the years. During slavery, those who worked in the master's house or the big house, received many favors. Some claimed fame from their ancestor's notoriety. Others were the unsung heroes. They worked the fields, laid the railroads, built houses, cities and highways. They received few favors. They were the ordinary people.

Such a man was **Alfred Robinson**, my grandfather. He was born February 5, 1868 on the Robinson plantation in Desoto County, Mississippi. He was the third son of **Redding and Ann Staple Robinson.**

Alf and three of his siblings married, and had families with children. His other siblings were farmers on the land with Paul, his younger brother. Alf and Luke chose to strike out on their own.

Alf was a quiet, tall, thin man who worked as a farmer and handy man. He could not read or write but stressed education to his children. He was a religious man who memorized many scriptures. He was an active member of Zion Hill Baptist Church. He was known for his prayers, the ability to keep peace and respect in the community. He died August 19, 1939. He was the father of eight children.

He married Ida Warren, who was born September 27, 1878. Ida worked as a cook and washerwoman. She died May 21, 1955.

Alf had the flu in 1918 and the doctor told Ida to prepare for his burial. My mother remembers him recovering and sitting in bed singing, *"I love the Lord, He heard my cry"*. God was the center of his life. He passed this love to his family, church and friends. He knew God always answered his prayers. It did not mean the answer was as he desired, but he listened and was open to the answer: For God would take care of him.

His love and compassion was shown in the way he lived. He opened his home to the less fortunate. I heard the story of Sarah, a homeless woman, who drifted from place to place with her young son in the small town. When no one was willing to take them in, my grandparents opened their home to them. Her son who is now a successful professional, frequently mentions the love and care received in their home.

Alf knew trouble is ever present in our lives. Today's society stresses a trouble free world. We must have no problem: a drug and/or alcohol for everything. If you're sad, take a picker upper; if you want a high, take a downer. But we must realize we will have trouble—but it won't last always. We must remember our heritage, rooted in the spiritual. Everything we do is tempered with our belief in God. For God is with us, no matter what the test.

Alf was quiet and unassuming, whereas Ida was assertive and talkative. They complimented each other, he tall and thin, she short and plump, he dark and handsome, she fair and pretty. They loved people and their house was always open to family, friends and ministers. There were never strangers in their midst.

Let us remember and reverence this ordinary man, who was a child of the real King. He left a legacy, a strong Faith in God, the love of family, church, friends, a compassionate spirit and the wisdom to know what is important in life.

The children of **Alf and Ida Warren Robinson** were:

Delia (Robert Jackson): She had one daughter, Robert D. Jackson. She had 4 (four) children.

Alberta: She was the first child of Ida Warren Robinson. She died at the age of 4 (four).

William: He was a Postal worker and father to one child, **Johnnie B. Robinson.**

> **Johnnie B.** married Robert Love and they became the parents of 7 (seven) children:
> **Peggy Forrest.** Peggy's two sons are:
> **Eric and Guy**
> **Robert**
> **Michael**
> **Wilford** He is the father of 2 (two) children.
> **Cynthia** She is the mother of (two) children.
> **Judy**
> **Johnny** He is the father of 1 (one) child.

Erma: She died at the age of 12 (twelve).

Lucille: She married Lonnie Saulsberry. Lucille became a school teacher and worked as an Assistant in a physician's office. She was the mother to one child, **Lonnie Mae.**

> **Lonnie Mae** married James Archie and they were parents to 7 (seven) children.
> **Janet** is the mother to 1 (one) child.

Ronald is the father of 3 (three) children.

James is the father of 1 (one) child

George

Alfred

Cynthia is the mother of 2 (two) children:

Kevin and Christian

Kimberly is the mother of 2 (two) children.

Idee: She married Simon Garrison and became a school teacher. She is the mother of (two) children:

William and Tommie.

William Alfred died in infancy.

Tommie J., aka "TJ" married Dorothy Moss. They are the parents to 5 (five) daughters:

Carolyn is married to James Walker. She is a school teacher and minister with two children:

Danielle (boutique owner)

Darrell

Elizabeth Ann married Wayne Weaver. She is a school teacher and the mother of three (3).

Shane

Shayde

Wayne, Jr. (DJ)

Gwendolyn is married to Purcell. She is a school teacher, entrepreneur. She has 3 children:

Tommy

Christopher

Evan

Sandra is a nurse practitioner and the mother of 4 (four) children:

Lakeshia

Jeremy

Jeffery

Tielina

Toni is married to Julius Savage and employed with the US Army Corps of Engineers. She is a minister with one child:

AdriAnna

Mattie: She married Rufus "Buster" Jenkins and was a school teacher and factory worker. They had two children, **Rutha** and **Inez**. Mattie was later married to Fred Cruse. There were no children born to this union.

Rutha B. is married to Willie L. (Bill) Jones. She is a registered nurse and author.

They are the parents of three children: **William, Linda and Timothy.**

William is married to Jackie Mayfield. He is the pastor of a United Methodist Church, owner of an Insurance agency and has one child:

Alexis

Linda is married to James Paley. She is the co-pastor of Spirit of Deliverance Center. She was previously married to Gregory Walter, Sr. There were 3 (three) children born of this union:

Gregory, Jr., Isaiah and Justin:

Gregory Theo has 2 (two) children:

Zamariah and Sariah

Isaiah

Justin (1 child)

Jaycee

Timothy was married to **Stephanie Brown**. There was one child born to this union. Timothy is the father of 11 (eleven) children:

Timothy, Jr. has 2 (two) children

Pebbles has 5 (five) children

Terrell has 3 (three) children

Aaron has 3 (three) children

Cattara

Marquizz

Timberly

Zuri

Zion

Ivory

Je'Kory

Inez was married to Emmett Payne (deceased). She is a practical nurse and entrepreneur (owner of several record shops and a touring bus company).

They have three children:

Michael, Kenneth and David.

Michael was married to Diane. They have a son, **Michael, Jr. and daughter, Demetria**

Michael Jr. has one child

Demetria has three (3) children.

Kenneth married Lacretia.

David is the father of (1) child:

T. Ebonee

<u>**Warren**</u>: He was married to Fannie Tolliver. There were 2 (two) children born from this union,

Warren Isaac and Charlotte.

Warren Isaac is a business owner in the Chicago area. He is married to Kathleen Woodville. To this union were born 4 (four) children:

Cozette has one child.

Annette

Warren Isaac, Jr. He is the father of two children.

Paulett

Charlotte has one son.

Dwight

The Robinson Family Home

MATTIE ROBINSON JENKINS CRUSE: THE STRENGTH TO ENDURE

'She is strong and respected and not afraid of the future. She speaks with gentle wisdom. She is always busy and looks after her family needs. Her children show their appreciation and her husband praises her. He says, "Many women are good wives, but you are the best of them all." Charm is deceptive and beauty disappears, but a woman who honors the LORD should be praised. Give her credit for all she does. She deserves the respect of everyone.'—Proverbs 25-31

My mother was chosen the honored Sunday School Teacher at Pilgrim Rest Baptist Church in 1989. She was in her late seventies. My sister and I were thrilled that she was honored. This is our tribute to her.

Mother was named after her aunt Matilda, called Til and Tilly, who was born a slave. Mattie comes from the name Matilda, which means *"maiden of valor".* Valor is a French word meaning to be strong, having the strength of mind or a spirit that enable a person to encounter danger with firmness. She provided music to our souls. I remember her singing *"The Lord will make a Way, Somehow"* as she went about her daily tasks. This became our motto or theme, especially after our parents divorced. Her music was able to charm and instill confidence in us. She was a good manager. With limited income, she provided for us. She helped us to see how *if we trust in God first, God would help us manage.*

Mother accepted her lot in life. She stressed: *"make yourself content, whatever your circumstance, do what is necessary and move on".* I think of her as tall, firm and steadfast with deep roots in family and church. She was thrifty, using whatever was available. She made pies out of Irish potatoes and tomatoes, whatever was in the pantry.

She was thankful for God's blessings. Her independence is an inspiration to us. After the divorce, she refused help from others (friends, family and the Welfare System). We would survive. She had the ability to bounce back with her calm, composed countenance.

Mattie was assertive, never left you wondering where she stood on an issue. She brought joy and delight into our lives. We recall her laughter and humor as we sat on the porch listening to her recite poems and tell stories, recalling happy times. She stressed, *"You are somebody, God's child from the Robinson and Jenkins families."*

This gray haired lady lives on Silver Street. She was brow beaten and stretched to her fullest, without bending or giving in. She kept the faith. From our mother, a tower of strength we learned to lift up God and self: Love, Laugh and Live. After a short illness at age 88 she died from congestive heart failure.

In her late 50's Mattie decided she wanted to own her own house. She became obsessed and spent all of her time looking at houses. Bill and I were in France. My sister wrote that she was afraid MaDear was losing her mind. Mother started buying a house on Silver Street. It was a four room, dilapidated shack. I was appalled when I saw the house, but Mother was excited over the possibilities. She planted flowers in the small yard. It took years, but she transformed the small shack into a modest home.

When they first married, Daddy had tried to teach her to drive. She ran off the road and he belittled her and she never tried to drive again. When she turned 60 and retired due to illness she decided she needed a car. We were amazed when she bought an old Chevrolet, passed the driver's test and drove all over Memphis. She drove her friends to various church meetings, to Hernando and other small nearby towns.

Mother was a cheerful and determined woman. I never thought of her as a fighter but she would not tolerate unpleasant situations. She laughed and said *"I won't marry again"* seemingly I like the same type man strong and good provider. She had great courage to continue to attend church and family functions after many lies and innuendos. The giving of her children by the court to Daddy was the ultimate blow. Her faith in God and the support of her family sustained her.

CHURCH

At the age of twelve, I went to the Mourners' Bench. On the third night I made my declaration of accepting Jesus as my Lord and Savior. I was baptized and joined East Trigg Church. Dr. W. H. Brewster, the pastor, was a great preacher and song writer. He was famous in the forties for his songs and poetry.

My parents divorced when I was thirteen, and the move to South Memphis was very traumatic. I joined Bloomfield Baptist Church at Mother's insistence. Mother was active as usual, singing in the choir, Sunday school and attending all services at 11:00 am, 3:00 pm, and many times the 7:00 pm services. I was angry and refused to participate, especially to play the piano. I have lived to regret this decision. I was sad over the changes in our lives: I missed the visits to our grandparents and my father's presence. I thought I was a daddy's girl, for he let me be me. My mother tried to make me do what was expected. I was searching for the meaning of life and studied the Bible extensively.

The negative expressions of my father kept coming to mind: "They only want your money." and "The preachers and deacons are having sex with the members." He mocked the preachers: 'he would grab his ear, rub his stomach, wipe his face and moan' and would say, *"Shout! Shout you (words He inserted) sob, dog, cat, mule, bastard, etc., Um _____m you!"* He would say the members never heard what was said, for they were looking for an emotional high.

I listened intently to preachers' messages and was mindful of actions of church people. Most of my first year in Washington, I sporadically attended chapel on the campus. During my second year I visited many churches. I frequently visited Berean Baptist. They wrote mother a letter of my visits. She was so happy.

I was impressed with the delivery of the sermon, no screaming or talking out. I heard every word and I began to grow spiritually. I was looking for a teaching minister, like Dr. Brewster.

When Bill was in the Air Force, we attended ecumenical services. I grew more while listening to ministers from different denominations. When we returned from his military tour, we started looking for a church home. Bill grew up actively involved in Mt. Zion Baptist Church, a small church on Georgia Avenue. He was regular in attendance at Sunday school and worship. He was very impressed with the Sunday school superintendent. In college, he was active with the Baptist Student Union. The director, Mr. Grimstead, was his mentor.

We visited many churches, mostly Baptist, with teaching preachers, the congregation was too large. Mother was concerned after eight months that we had not joined a church. She suggested we visit a small new church on Gill and Pillow Streets. We visited and were impressed with the warm fellowship and sincerity of the Pastor, the Rev. A. E. Andrews. Rev. Andrews was a dedicated, sincere man, not a fiery preacher with any outward frills or piety. He was an excellent teacher, someone I could respect. We attended the new members' class, where he taught Bible, polity of the Presbyterian Church and stewardship.

PORCHES

As I walked to and from the cleaners, I reflected on porches. I remember the porches of my grandparents:

The farmhouse in Moore town, of the Jenkins, was elevated off the ground so air, chickens and dogs could go underneath, and six steps led to the front porch which ran the length of the house. On the porch were handmade chairs, a swing and two long benches. In the evenings and on Sunday's after church, we sat on the porch, listened to stories, drank lemonade ate tea cakes. This large porch was needed for twelve children and many grandchildren. The back porch, which ran the length of the kitchen was used as an extension or added room. An elevated shelf held the water bucket, dipper and wash basin. A clothes line ran from post to post and held wash clothes and towels. A churn and a homemade bench lined one wall. This was the work area, for churning, washing of hand items, feeding the chickens and preparing fruits or vegetables for dinner or canning.

My Robinson grandparents' home, in the town of Hernando, was low and on the ground. The front porch was the length of the house, wide and boxed in, with only one step. This step was used as an extra seat. A swing was the only permanent piece of furniture and was usually occupied by my grandmother and a grandchild or a visitor. The four grandchildren, who spent part of each summer in Hernando, clamored to sit in the swing with Mama Ida. Straight chairs were brought from the kitchen as needed for Mama Ida's three sisters, relatives and friends who visited often. The small screened side porch led to the kitchen, breakfast and supper were sometimes eaten here. Mama Ida did washing and ironing for white families and the side porch was used to sort and fold clothes. In my child's mind these porches denoted the financial status of my grandparents, as their porches were much larger than ours.

In 1937, our first home in Memphis had no porch. My parents rented two rooms of a four room duplex, located on the corner of Washington and McNeil on an alley. From the rear four steps led into a kitchen and bedroom. There was little time for sitting on porches. Daddy was gone all day and many times into the night. Mother was busy also, working a half day for the white lady on the corner of McNeil and Court. She had problems adjusting the gas stove and I remember the charred toast she bought home every day. I still like charred toast and frequently burn bread. In the evenings, Mother sat on the steps and talked to the lady next door and other neighbors as we played in a small grassless area. I don't remember this as our individual yard, as it was used as a pathway for everyone who rented in the rear.

In 1939, Daddy rented a white bungalow house from Aunt Inez, located at 1385 Hemlock, with a nice front porch the length of the front room. The porch was an added room used for sleeping by our extended family, uncles, and cousins from Hernando. I started to school from this house.

In 1940, my parents purchased the house next door, 1389 Hemlock, a three and one half room house. It had a small front porch, right on the ground and an even smaller back porch with a toilet taking up most of the space. The back of the house was elevated. This is the house I think of as 'home'. Daddy was into trucking, public hauling and farm labor. Because our porch was small, we sat under a big oak tree in the yard and listened to the stories from our parents and extended family.

In 1946, Mother and Daddy separated and Mother moved in with Cousin Jane at 84 W. Trigg, a grey four room bungalow with a porch the length of one room and four steps. It was one of two houses sandwiched in between the Wabash Screen Door Company and Sam's Grocery. I spent my teen years sitting on the porch with my sister, people watching and making up stories. I imagined the fun they had going to the movies, the clubs down the street, dances and sporting activities.

I have come full circle, sitting on my porch that is the length of two rooms. Right now, nothing is on the porch. As a retired person, how will I use this porch, pleasure or practical? People in this neighborhood rarely sit on front porches. What would happen if I started sitting on the porch?

SISTERS

When I think of sisters, I think of my mother and her sisters. For many years we went to Hernando most Sundays and all holidays. After Mama Ida's death, the sisters seemed to grow even closer. Mother and Aunt Lucille called each other every day. Aunt Lucille was an early riser and called my mother, Mattie, between 4:30 a.m. and 5:00 a.m. Mother was a late sleeper and after retirement she tried to get Aunt Lucille to call at a later time. This was to no avail; she continued to call early. They also called Aunt Idee once a week. The importance of family came from their father, Alf. Everyone who had any connection or a drop of Robinson blood was considered kin. Therefore, I thought everyone in Hernando was kin, as many with the last name were from the Robinson or Robertson plantation. The importance of this kinship was stressed at all gatherings. Whenever there was sickness, no matter the difficulty, the sisters were there. The sisters never left a sick person's home or hospital. We (nieces or nephew} could not explain to our spouses and children why this was so important to them. I now find I'm doing the same thing. How many bed sides and funerals I have attended because of these sisters, who stressed: *"Remember your kin."*

Aunt Lucille, the oldest girl, was the second of seven children of Alfred and Ida Robinson. She was a quiet, dignified person who dressed every day as if going to work or church. She wore lipstick, rouge, powder and jewelry; sometimes two or three strings of beads and bracelets. She said the bracelets worn on her wrist and ankles were to ward off rheumatism. She taught school in Mississippi for many years. Lucille was a tall, thin, dark-skinned woman, who always carried herself in a dignified manner. She was very knowledgeable with a warm, gentle smile. She was a Bible scholar and a Sunday school teacher, with a strong conviction of right and wrong.

Aunt Lucille had strong feeling against birth control pills. She thought they were used as a means of killing off blacks, and as family was important to her, the more children the better. Her house was always available to the needy. It served as a safe haven for the children in the community. She encouraged education but stressed the many ways to become educated. She always stated to: *"use your experience to gain knowledge and a bad experience to make a positive change in your life"*.

Many were surprised when she married Lonnie Saulsberry, a sporty man. He worked at a local funeral home and sold whiskey and gambled to add to his livelihood. To this union one daughter, Lonnie Mae, was born. Lucille and Lonnie divorced after fourteen years. She moved to Memphis and later married Joseph Williams.

We were sitting on the porch drinking beer and coolers when Aunt Lucille passed down the history of the craving and inability of the Robinsons to drink alcohol. She named the Robinson men who had problems with alcohol, but also told of the good side of each one, like: *"William is a heavy drinker, but he never misses a day of work".* She also told us of the high blood pressure and heart trouble that runs in the Robinson line. Aunt Lucille died at age seventy six of congestive heart failure.

Aunt Idee, the fifth child, was outgoing with a beautiful smile. Two girls died between her and Aunt Lucille. She and her brother William helped with the plowing and hard work on the farm. Her house was the gathering place for friends and relatives in Hernando. She and her husband, Simon (Bo) Garrison bought land adjoining Grandpa Alf and Mama Ida's place. She had two sons, William Albert, who died in infancy. Her aunt, Matilda, (Till) Robinson Love said on the birth of her second son, Tommy Joyernal (T.J.). *"This child will live, the other one was too pretty to live".* The first child was fair skinned with black curly hair. Many times fair-skinned and wavy hair, were considered good looking. Aunt Idee looked like their mother, fair and plump. She was a hard worker, taught school during the season and hauled farm laborers to the Delta. For many years, the school year was split. School sessions were scheduled around the chopping and picking of cotton. When she and her sisters started teaching, a degree was not necessary, and as the criteria changed, she kept going to school. She drove to Holly Springs on Saturdays and went to Summer school off and on for many years. Her perseverance paid off and she obtained a BA degree.

She and Bo, a mechanic, had a good life. After his death, and after many years as a widower, she married Walter (Dock) Mathis. He was a farmer, who owned many acres of land. This marriage lasted only a few years. She moved back to Hernando and they divorced.

Aunt Idee was my favorite aunt, she never preached to us. She always said, *"I'm just straight with you."* She always listened and let us makes our own decisions. I remember a summer when I was in my forties, my children were teenagers, and Bill and I had grown apart. He was always busy working and never had time to attend activities with me. He always seemed to want others around us. I felt old, fat and not needed. When I confronted Bill about our lack of time together, he said, *"I thought with your involvement in church, music, volunteer activities, work and the children, all you need or want from me is to provide money."* I was very hurt, but could not express my feelings. I took off from work and went to visit Aunt Idee. She greeted me and could tell by my expression, something was wrong. She never asked me, *"What's wrong?"* she just hugged me and started cooking one of her famous meals. For three days we ate, slept and sat on the porch. As people passed by, either walking or driving, they waved and many times stopped and chatted. Many of them knew my mother and father and had known me as a child. I don't remember any exact words spoken, but everything reminded me

I was special and important. On the third day, I told her how I felt and what Bill had said. She listened and sipped her drink. After a while, I decided to work on my marriage. Aunt Idee taught for over fifty (50) years, was active and remained in her house until her death at ninety-seven (97) years of age.

Mattie, my mother, was the baby of the family for nine years before the birth of her brother, Warren. She was tall, thin with a dark brown complexion. She would always retain this baby position in the family. She was the outgoing one, the first to marry and the first to divorce. She was not afraid to venture out. In her day, many women stayed in marriages, especially if the man was a good provider. It didn't matter if he was abusive or a womanizer. She loved to dance and recite poetry. In the family, she was often called on to pantomime poems and stories. Her sisters always catered to her, because to them, she was the pretty baby sister.

She married Daddy, Rufus (Buster) Jenkins, Jr. in May 1931. I was born January 1933 and my sister, Inez in 1935. His parents owned many acres of land, and Daddy had a 1929 Ford. So it was considered that she married "well". Mama's Ida's sisters, Lula and Rosie, were teachers and helped and encouraged their nieces to become teachers. Mother taught school for a few years in the Delta, before my birth. Many times the church and school were in the same building. The trustees of the church gave approval for hiring the teachers. The teachers stayed in homes in the area and returned to their homes on the weekend.

When they moved to Memphis, Daddy started transporting field laborers. He and Mother chopped and picked cotton. She sold drinks and homemade pies. They left home about 4:00 a.m. in the dark and returned at night. They were able to buy the house next door, 1389 Hemlock Street. During the war years, mother worked at Firestone Tire and Rubber Company. After fifteen years, she and Daddy divorced. After the divorce, she worked as a maid, factory worker and hospital worker. Three years after the divorce, she married Fred Cruse. This marriage lasted three years. She continued with her church work, singing in the choir, teaching Sunday school and working with the mission board. She organized a social club, The Veterans Wives Club and Associates.

In her late fifties (50s), Mother decided she wanted to own her house. She became obsessed and spent all of her time looking at houses. Bill and I were in France. My sister wrote and said she was afraid MeDear was losing her mind. Mother started buying a house on Silver Street. It was a four room dilapidated shack. I was appalled when I saw the house, but Mother was excited over the possibilities. She had planted flowers in the small yard. It took years, but she transformed the small shack into a modest home. When she turned sixty and had retired due to illness, she decided she needed a car. Daddy had tried to teach her to drive when they first married. She had run off the road and he belittled her and she never tried to drive again. We were amazed when she bought an old Chevrolet, passed the driver's test and drove all over Memphis. She drove her friends to various churches, club meetings, to Hernando and other nearby small towns.

Mother was a cheerful and determined woman. I never thought of her as a fighter, but she would not tolerate unpleasant relationships. She laughed and said, "I won't marry again. Seemingly, I like the same type man, strong and good providers. But they are the same regardless of their color, high yellow or charcoal black." For her to continue to attend church and family functions after many lies and innuendos, took great courage. The giving of her children, by the court, to Daddy, was the ultimate blow. Her faith in God and the support of her family sustained her.

After a short illness, she died at the age of 88, from congestive heart failure.

AUNT LULAS PRAYER

My earliest memory of prayer is from the old rural churches of Second Baptist Church in Hernando and Pleasant Hill Baptist Church of Moore town, Mississippi. These are the churches of my grandparents. Although we lived in Memphis, my parents kept their rural roots. We returned frequently to these churches. Mother taught me to pray by example. Her teachers were my maternal grandfather, Alf Robinson, and my paternal grandmother, Lula Jenkins.

Mother didn't want me to have an experience such as she had as a newlywed. She tells the story of going to church with the Jenkins women. She was accustomed to a structured service where the deacons or Mothers of the church were the only one called on to pray, extemporaneously. When the old deacon called *"Sister Jenkins"* and pointed to her, she closed her eyes, hoping he would point toward her mother-in-law. He soon called, *"Sister Buster Jenkins"*. Buster was my father's nickname. She was trembling so hard the pew was shaking. Her sister-in-law, Lula called "Sis A", knelt down and prayed. Lula's prayer was similar to this prayer:

"O God, it's once more and again, your humble servant bows
To praise your name…Praise your Holy name!
God of Abraham, Jacob and Isaac, You have been with us through all
generations. You are a good God, You woke me up this morning!
Clothed in my right mind, with a reasonable portion of health and strength,
To a day I've never seen before, with all its beauty…Thank you, Lord.
I could be resting on my cooling board. Thank you, God.
You fed me with food and cooling water, gave me a place to stay.
Thank you, Lord. I could hear the birds, frogs and the wind
rustling through the trees. Thank you, Lord. Lord, we want
you to come in this room, for we have many needs.
You know us all by name. We pray for all the sick
and those who are less fortunate.
We pray for Brother Lonzo White and Sister Bertha Gray.
Touch their hot and feverish brow. Soothe and move that pain, if it be your will.
Help those who don't know you as a Savior and pardoner of sins.
Touch Lord! Protect us from dangers, seen and unseen.

And when this feeble body is worn out, can't study war no
more, receive me unto Thine kingdom, I pray.
This is Your servant's prayer, in Jesus' Name,
Amen.

Prayers followed a pattern of praise, admiration, and thanksgiving, and could last from 15 to 20 minutes, with responses of *"Thank You, Lord"*, from the congregation. Sometimes a burst of song was heard. It was a personal prayer, with names of people who needed prayer. You couldn't always name the dangers or problems, due to segregation and Jim Crow laws. So, they prayed of the seen and unseen dangers. They acknowledged death as a normal cycle of life and their belief of the hereafter.

From these prayers I learned to know God as a personal God, who is concerned about me and my problems and one who answers prayer. I am aware of the seasons of life and know that nothing lasts forever. When trouble comes, and it will come, I know, this too, will pass away; and at the end, I have a home waiting for me.

BAE'S REFLECTIONS

"I thank God for every remembrance of you." is one of my favorite scriptures. Prayer is a vital part of my life. I praise and glorify God with each breath. My prayers are mostly prayers of Thanksgiving, for God has been so good to me. I feel his divine intervention has been present in my life, guiding me to heights and places I could not imagine. These reflections help me to determine who I am.

I remember and reverence a special, but ordinary man whose name was Alf. He was my grandfather and a Child of the King, the real King. He left me a legacy of a strong faith in God, love of family, church and friends, hospitality, a compassionate spirit and the wisdom of knowing what is important in life.

PART 1

LIVING AND BLESSED

1933–1946

"TO DREAM THE IMPOSSIBLE DREAM"

**TO DREAM THE IMPOSSIBLE DREAM;
TO FIGHT THE UNBEATABLE FOE!**

WE SURVIVED

Lord you are worthy of praise, all glory and honor I give to you. I thank you for your goodness throughout the ages. Thank you for bringing my ancestors to these shores. THEY SURVIVED. They endured slavery and the selling of family members to other locations. THEY SURVIVED.

Thank you for my great-grandfather who in 1867 walked from southern Mississippi and caught rides to the Cub Lake area, looking and searching for his sister, Dorcas. THEY SURVIVED.

Thank you Almighty God for my parents who made it in city life and the big depression. They made jobs. They provided transportation for farm laborers and sold homemade pies. THEY SURVIVED.

O Eternal God, I pray for our families today. HELP US SURVIVE.

Our men...sons, brothers, husbands...so many are unemployed; in jail, on drugs or mentally ill. They are unable to support their families. These young men have no role models. Their Fathers are not in the homes or do not provide child support. HELP LORD.

Our women...daughters, sisters, mothers, grandmothers...They are so vulnerable, living in areas with toxic waste, many with chronic diseases. There are many who are the only ones in the family working. There are those who are working long hours and are unable to attend school functions. There are mothers who are infected with HIV, sick, tired, pushing on.

Our Grandmothers are caring for their grandchildren. Many of them are depending on unemployment benefits, food stamps and Medicaid. LORD, HEAR OUR PRAYER.

Many of our families have no voice. No one listens to them. HELP LORD. We must be the voice for the voiceless. We must write letters to our congressmen. We must write to the office of Public Witness and other church or public papers. Lord, give us the strength and courage to endure. We have Hope and Faith that You will be with our families as you have in the past and WE WILL SURVIVE. AMEN.

MY FIRST REMEMBRANCE

I was born in Hernando, Mississippi at my maternal grandparent's home, delivered by a midwife. Hernando is located 25 miles from Memphis, Tennessee, and is the county seat of DeSoto County. In the 1930's, it was typical of small southern towns. *"Separate but Equal"* was the slogan of this time period. The town square was the center of activity. The main street circled the courthouse with highway 51 as the outside perimeter. The square included a bank, grocery store, law office, hardware/clothing store, grocery store and funeral home. The economy was dependent on cotton and the rulers were the wealthy plantation owners. In this town everything revolved around Banks and Company. Moore Town, about 10 miles west of Hernando, was a community of 8 to 10 black families. It consisted of one small store, owned by Mr. Moore, a white man. Blacks referred to the area by the church's name, Pleasant Hill.

My first remembrance: I am 4 years old playing under a large oak tree with my sister, Inez, age 2 and my Uncle Leroy, age 5. We are playing with spools and a carved horse made for Leroy by one of his older brothers. It's a bright sunny day, hot and dry. Our dusty hair is plaited in many small braids, dresses made out of flowered cotton sacks. The *"White washed"* house sits on a hill about 30 yards off the main road. The inclining drive circles the big oak tree and goes past the house and barn to three small houses on the back lot. The fenced— in front yard is filled with many colorful flowers. No grass is visible and there is no formal design to the flower garden. To the right of the house and *"out house"* is an apple orchard and to the left the garden patch. Everyone is busy, the adults and older children are in the cotton field. In the morning they go to the field farthest from the house. My paternal grandmother, Lula, is busy cooking dinner (the noon meal). She will go to the closest field in the afternoon. This seems like such a peaceful scene, but something is wrong. Where is Mother? Mother had left my Father and returned to her parents in town. This would be a frequent occurrence of my childhood.

Trouble was a mainstay of our life. I can hear daddy singing the blues, *"Trouble in Mind, I'm Blue"* and mother singing a church song, *"I'm so glad trouble don't last always"*. This is the story of my life: the joys and sorrows, and trouble.

LEAVING MISSISSIPPI

Under the cover of darkness, on a cold spring night, we left Mississippi. It's a cold night in April 1937. The only light comes from a few stars and the quarter moon. We stayed on the deeply rutted gravel back roads until we passed Rabbit's Ridge. Then the truck bounced up to Highway 51.

I sensed Mother was scared as I smelled her pungent sweaty odor. She is holding my sister in her lap and I'm snuggled close to her warm body. When we saw car lights approaching mother would look back frantically. There was little talking. It's as if we are all holding our breath. Mother has many reasons to fear. She is leaving her family and the small town where she knows everyone for the big city life with no friends or family: from the segregated, paternalistic society, where she knew what was expected, to the unknown. She fears but loves her husband. When we cross the TN state line, mother relaxed and became talkative and inquisitive. As we passed through the night the trees seemed to bend and sigh and say: *"Why? Why? Why?"*

Cousin Josie, Mr. Sam, her friend, Mother, Inez and I are tightly squeezed in the cab of a small pick-up truck. All of our belonging, two beds with mattresses, a small chest, handmade table and four chairs, dishes, two pots, cast iron skillet, jars of canned fruits and vegetables, a salt cured ham, four quilts and clothes are packed in the back. My sister and I are wearing flower sack dresses made by our fraternal grandmother: baggy sweaters, long cotton stockings and sturdy shoes. We are covered with a patch work quilt. Mother asks the question, *"Why? Why? Why?"*

Mother met Daddy at 2nd Baptist Church when he asked a friend to introduce them. He was twenty one years old with his own car. He was light skinned with tightly coiled reddish brown hair, 5 feet and 11 inches, but appears taller. He had a cocky walk. Mother says like a rooster. They eloped in 1931. He was obsessed with work and making money. He was temperamental and domineering. Most of the time, Mother could not please him. He states she's lazy, does not know how to cook or care for babies. He has always worked, starting when he was eight years old, keeping his younger brother, Earnest. He must have his way and expects people to cater to his wishes. He and Mother argue often, he's verbally abusive and they separate frequently.

After their marriage, Daddy was a sharecropper for a year. Then they moved to Hernando and he worked for the Works Projects Administration (WPA), helping to build Highway 51. He quit working for the WPA when they left the area. He began *bootlegging, selling and delivering'* corn liquor. He was never arrested, as he eluded the sheriff. He'd go in hiding, many times in Memphis, staying for a week or more before returning. In the early spring of 1937, the white owner of the adjoining farm told his father the sheriff planned to kill him when he returned.

It's amazing how news traveled without telephones or letters. The message was given to a person going to town, who informed Mother. In this small town, African Americans knew someone in every family. Mother's brother, Warren, went to the bus station. He gave the message to a woman going to Memphis, who told a man standing on the corner of Highway 51 and Parkway, who told Aunt Inez and she told Daddy. So, we joined the exodus of the Great Migration, of people leaving farms and small towns, who were looking for jobs or running from the law. We fled north—to Memphis.

WASHINGTON BOTTOM

We lived briefly with Cousin Josie in North Memphis. Then we moved to Washington Bottom. This area is located near Popular and Cleveland. The eight (8) gray duplexes with no front yard consisted of three (3) rooms on each side. We entered from the rear as we rented the kitchen and middle room. The house was located beside an alley. This gave Daddy room for his truck and vegetable bins.

During our second week on Washington Street, I went to the store with Annie one of the older girls. My eyes popped at the sight of large glass jars filled with cookies, candy and pickles. I made my first purchase, two cookies for a penny. I walked out eating my cookies, leaving Annie behind. I was fascinated with the large manicured green lawns. I became alarmed and started crying when it started getting dark and I noticed Annie was not with me. A lady came from one of the big houses and called the police. The white policeman, thin, tall with dark wavy hair knelt down to my level. With a twinkle in his eyes, he promised me an ice cream cone if I would stop crying. I couldn't believe my good fortune: cookies and ice cream! I was returned home, thirty (30) minutes after my parents reported me missing. This experience left me with a positive image of policemen as helpers. Because I was able to tell the policeman my name, *"nickname"* and last name, Daddy decided I was smart.

GRANPA'S DEATH

My first experience with death occurred in 1937. Daddy came home with a perplexed, forlorn look. Mother immediately asked, *"What's wrong, is Papa dead?"* Daddy was amazed and couldn't believe mother knew what he was struggling with, and how to tell her. This bears out mother's claim to her premonitions of death in her family.

My maternal grand parents' home started as a room on each side of a dog trot. A large kitchen and three rooms were added as the family increased. There was a stepdown from the original rooms. The bed was removed from the front room and grandpa's casket placed in front of the fireplace. During the *"wake",* someone was in the room with the body at all times. The house was full of people, coming and going, with mothers' sisters and brothers, uncles, aunts, cousins and other relatives. Food and drinks were plentiful, brought by neighbors and friends who also took turns sitting with the body. In the other rooms everyone told remembrances of Grandpa. Mother's younger brother and friends were outside drinking moonshine (corn whiskey). I don't remember much about the funeral. But at the burial I can still hear the dirt hitting the wooden box and see the horse drawn carriage with the coffin.

I never remember being told *"I love you"* by my parents or grandparents, but I knew I was loved. I was their second grandchild, a girl. They were not demonstrative or verbal. They made clothes and toys for us. I played with miniature farm animals, scooters, wheelbarrows and dolls, all handmade. My maternal grandmother was a little more demonstrative, showing how glad she was to see me.

SUMMERS IN HERNANDO

Soon after the last day of school, we went to Hernando for the summer for one month with our maternal grandmother, Mama Ida; and one month with our paternal grandparents, Rufus and Lula, *"Grampa and Mama Lula"*, at the farm. Lonnie Mae and TJ, our cousins were our constant companions. Every morning after breakfast, TJ, Inez and I, went to the West End to Lonnie Mae's grandmother, Mama Ada. She was another excellent cook. The West End was the action area for blacks. It consisted of one section of one street. I don't remember the street name, but it was around the bend after Grandmama Lizzie's house, my great grandmother (Mama Ida's mother). From Aunt Lula's, Mama Ida's sister, to the next bend were three cafes, one to ten small houses, and a funeral home. Everything was colorless, no paint on the buildings, dirt yards, no flowers, old tires, garbage, puddles of water with dogs and small children who were running around in different stages of dress. Ms. Mary Etta's café was at a bend in the road and an intersection of a road, on a hill. The café was one room with a counter and two to three small tables and a kitchen. To the left of one room was an additional large room that was the length of the room and kitchen. The floor was covered with dirt and saw dust and in one corner was a juke box (aka Sea-Berg), that played 20 songs of R&B, blues music.

I loved going to the West End. This is where I learned to dance. On Saturday nights this was the place to be: there was music, whiskey and dancing! The county was a dry county (no alcohol). This was an exciting place for young girls and boys. There was much fussing and fighting and it seems as if nothing has changed with the killing of young men, accidents and domestic squabbles. Therefore, we were not allowed on the West End after dark.

We enjoyed the freedom of riding bicycles over the small town, meeting other children and racing bicycles. Another thing we did was to find small animals and birds to kill with a sling shot. After riding our bikes in the morning, we would go back to the cafe and order hamburgers that were greasy, and the bread was soggy, lots of mustard, onions and mayonnaise… oh, the cholesterol! But how delicious! In the afternoons we went to the woods and gullies looking for small animals and birds. We would pull all the feathers we could get off the birds. Then we would grill them over a fire.

After the first of July we went to Moore Town to the farm. As we grew older, we wanted to stop going to the farm for everyone had to work. I got sick in the field, it was too hot, so I gathered black berries, plums etc. One of TJ's friends, Jimmy, drowned in a small lake: my second death remembrance.

REMEMBERANCES OF CHRISTMAS

As I ponder on remembrances of Christmas, where do I begin and what particular Christmas? My daddy was the first of his immediate family to leave the small town and rural area of northern Mississippi for a big city. We moved to Memphis in 1937, I was four years old, my sister Inez was two. In 1938, we moved to 1385 Hemlock Street between South Parkway East and Kerr, near Highway 51. Daddy's grandfather Sam, his Aunt Inez and Uncle Cortrell had moved to Memphis in the mid 20's, and lived on Hemlock Street. This area was then in the county.

My parents kept their rural roots and went back "down home" weekly. Our activities were centered around family in Hernando and Moore Town, Mississippi. For years the old churches were still our churches. The churches had Sunday worship two (two) to 3 (three) Sundays a month. Second Baptist, my maternal grandmother's church, met the first Sunday; Zion Hill Baptist church met on the second Sunday; Pleasant Hill Baptist, my paternal grandparents church, met the third Sunday; and Pleasant Grove CME church, my great grandparents' church met on the fourth Sunday. We attended one of these churches on Sundays at least three Sunday's a month. Many in the community made the rounds visiting different churches on their meeting Sunday.

Preparations for Christmas began on a cold day in November, with hog killing. My father and many of his brothers gathered on the farm, for this ritual, in preparation for winter and Christmas. Everyone worked including children: gathering kindling wood, making a fire, toting (carrying) water, killing the hogs, cutting up the meat, cleaning the meat, especially the chitterling, preserving the meat (salting) for the smoke house. I knew Christmas was not too far off as the grown-ups made plans for the New Year.

Christmas was a time for visiting, either on Christmas day or the second or third day. With two grandparents, a great grandmother, Daddy's two or three married brothers and sisters, we spent a lot of time visiting. As a child, I thought everyone in Hernando was our kindred. You were expected to eat at each house. I remember Aunt Clara's tea cakes and Aunt Inez's caramel cake, one for the goodness and exquisite taste, and the other for its tastelessness.

Mother prepared for Christmas by cleaning house. It started with the removal of soot from the walls and furniture which was caused by the wood and coal burning stoves. There would be the hanging of wall paper in the front room and the washing and stretching of curtains. Our front room was where we entertained visitors. It was furnished with a bed, a dresser with a bench, an arm chair and a small round table, and, a rag rug Daddy made. One time mother brought a bedspread from a traveling salesman. This was unknown to Daddy for he didn't allow a white person in our house. He and mother had a big argument. Daddy did all his transactions with whites on the corner of Bellevue and Parkway Streets.

MIDSOUTH FAIR

My first remembrance of the Fair was during the 1940's. My sister and I were going to the fair with Fate. Fate was an older cousin; he and his parents were staying with us. His father, Dewitt, was the first of many of my father's brothers who came to stay with us. We always had extended family with us. Many of these brothers, especially the younger ones were like brothers to me.

On a cool fall day, when I was 11 years old, I awoke with great expectations, thinking: *'This is the day, we're going to the fair'.* The fair for colored people started after the fair for whites ended. It was usually very cool or as I remember sometimes raining or overcast. After doing our Saturday morning chores: feeding the chickens, helping with the washing and hanging clothes on the clothes line; and, cleaning the front porch, which served as an extra room. Then between 10:00 am and 11:00 a.m., we were off. We walked from Parkway and Bellevue, to the fairgrounds (Airways and Southern Streets) about two miles. This was a big occasion for us as we rarely left the neighborhood, which was the side streets south of South Parkway and Bellevue (Highway 51) to Kerr, the southern border and College Street, the west boundary. I marveled at the houses, owned by prominent blacks on Parkway, as we walked north.

As we approached the fair, I could smell food and hear screaming, laughter and the noise of the crowd. We were excited and awed at the sights and sounds. We ran to ride the merry-go-round. This was the beginning of a wonderful experience. We rode the bumper cars, the whip, and the Ferris wheel. I had my first experience on a boat, the Old Mill and going through the Tunnel of Love. We had our first cotton candy, candied apples and hot dogs. These were novelties as Mother cooked only meat, vegetables and dessert. Fate had recently moved from the country. He was a 4H member (Future Farmers of America). He was interested in the pigs and cattle barn, and this became part of my experience. So, my fondest memories of the Mid-South Fair included rides, food and the cattle barn. I looked forward to attending the fair every year, and did so until I was fifteen. Then my interests changed, and I had no one to go with me or to take me.

During the 70's, I went to the Mid-South Fair with my children. Times had changed and the fair was desegregated and school children had a day off to attend. We went as a family and I was surprised my children were not afraid to ride the many rides, even the Pippen (roller coaster). They enjoyed seeing their Father try the games of chance: target shooting, guessing weights, etc. My parents were not able to attend the fair with us; they were too busy trying to make a living.

In the 1980's, I went to the Fair with my youngest son. He was afraid of the rides. To encourage him I went on the Pippen with him. He overcame his fear, but I didn't. I went yearly with him until he decided he didn't want to be seen with his mother, but no riding of the Pippen for me. We went to the Rodeo, haunted house and side shows. The smallest woman, the tallest man, and the alligator woman were common attractions. We visited the barn and the exhibits.

In the 1990's, my mother and I visited the fair each year. She was interested in the cattle barn. She especially enjoyed the quilts, flowers and canning. My church friend and mentor, Minnie Robinson entered floral arrangements and needlework. She checked to see how many ribbons she received. I've come full circle attending the fair as a senior citizen. I visited the exhibits, ate a little of the good smelling food and watched the crowd. I plan to visit the fair this year with my five year old granddaughter, as I have done with some of my other grandchildren…until they didn't want to be seen with their grandmother.

LOOKS

As a child I was never told how I looked. When people saw us they commented on my sister. They said, *"How pretty she is, and she looks like her aunt Inez."* Then they would turn and say to me: *"and you look just like your daddy."* No further comments. I thought this meant I looked like a boy. Mother and daddy never told us *"you're pretty"* or *"I love you"*. I sensed I was loved, but had no idea how I looked. How you looked was not important.

I remember my first job, working as a maid/assistant for two white doctors. I was told by the younger of the two not to wear red lipstick. I took this to mean my lips were too big to wear red lipstick. Since that time, as a rebellion, I always wear red lipstick.

We were admonished not to look like Cora. She was our unmarried aunt, Daddy's sister. As a young woman, she weighed over 300 pounds. She was over sixty years of age when she had her first boyfriend. After the death of her parents, she moved to Memphis and met this man. I had a fear that I would become another Cora, fat and unwed. She lived her life taking care of the family. As the oldest child, she cared for the other eleven children.

So the only reference to looks was weight. Since everyone worked in the field, none of the others were fat. I'm sure this was upsetting to Cora. My sister gained weight when she was ten years old. As a teenager, she lost it and has been very weight conscious all of her adult life.

Daddy rarely dressed up. He wore work clothes even on Sunday. He rarely went inside the church building. Looks were surely not important.

INDEPENDENCE

Children do what's expected of them. I can't remember when I heard about college but knew I would go. I was told to become self-sufficient, not to depend on a man. Me'Dear, now divorced, was working at Firestone Tire and Rubber Company. She rode the bus which meant she was up at 4:30 a.m., catching the bus at 5:45 a.m. Buses ran all night. This was the common means of transportation. Many friendships developed from meeting on the bus. Many people I know from South Memphis I met on the bus. We rarely visited—our entertainment was people watching. We sat on the porch and I made up the stories of the people passing by. Many of the church going people were all dressed up going to the seven churches in the area. All the churches were Baptist except for one small AME. The Church of God In Christ (COGIC) was just becoming known. My classmate, Barbara Jo's, father was a Bishop in the COGIC but none were in our neighborhood. I also imagined the good times the people had in the cafes. There was a cafe two doors from our house, one on the corner and another on Kansas Street. I watched on Friday and Saturday evenings as the women came in tight fitting dresses, eyes made up, hair in the latest styles. There was much hugging, loud profane language and laughing. We were admonished not to live this life—no meaning—just *"good timing"* life. I would have loved this happy appearing life, but I guess I was afraid of the consequences. I also knew this would hurt Mother. I always wanted to please Mother and Daddy.

Me'Dear met Mr. Fred while she worked at Firestone. He was a large dark- skinned man from the Lauderdale Subdivision. Everyone was identified from the section or neighborhood where they lived. He worked as a construction worker, was a sharp dresser and took Mother to the movies and musicals on Beale Street. They married and he moved into our house. I resented him from the beginning. No one could take my Daddy's place. Their marriage put the finality on Mother and Daddy's relationship. Mr. Fred had never been around children and thought Me'Dear was too protective of us. He had a low opinion of women and referred to them as sluts. He was upset because we didn't have jobs. I think Mother was afraid for us to venture out of the neighborhood. The jobs available were as maids or cafe workers. Many young girls were at the mercy of white men at these jobs. She was determined to give us the same benefits we would have had if she had stayed with Daddy. Therefore, she worked and we kept house and cooked. She said, *"I'll take care of them until they graduate from high school."* He often said, *"You will be wasting your time. They will be like all the others around here—sluts—no good."* This made me more determined to excel. ***"I'll show you—Fred Cruse. I'll be somebody. I won't have to ask you or any man for money."***

Daddy was to give us $20.00 a week. This was not a court order as we were supposed to still live with him. He married Mary and she didn't want us around or receiving any money. Many times when we went to get our money,

if she was home, he said he didn't have any money or would not mention it at all. I was too stubborn to ask. I said, *"He knows we need money"*. My sister, Inez, would sometimes go in and ask for money which she would receive. I guess I was afraid of rejection and I've always had trouble expressing strong emotions. Mother never talked down about Daddy. His strange ways were described as *"just Buster"*. She stressed his good points—his love of family and strong work ethic. Nothing was to stop us. We would grow up and be strong, self-sufficient women.

THE BROKEN SWAN

One of my fond memorable Christmases was the year I received three pink swans. I had medical problems and Pam Dickson, a student at Southwestern College (Rhodes), stayed with us to help with the children. She was the daughter I could have had early in our marriage and the older sister, Billy and Linda hoped for. She took Billy, ten (10) years old, and Linda, eight (8) years old and Timothy, age four (4) to Popular Plaza Shopping Center. The children were excited, their first time selecting a gift, using money they had saved. As they passed a store, they saw beautiful crystal animals. Billy and Linda spotted three pink swans, all different sizes. They agreed this was the perfect gift. They watched as the saleswoman wrapped them in tissue paper. Christmas morning they anxiously waited for me to open their gift. Alas, the smallest swan was broken. The children were heartbroken. I reassured them, I could fix it. I used super glue and the break wasn't easily seen, but you could feel the roughness.

Every time I looked at the broken swan, I think of God's love and how he mends our 'brokenness'. Whatever the problem, He is there: divorce, disappointments, addiction, and loss of jobs, to name a few. Sometimes you can't see where the break occurred, but we remain fragile. We must stay close to God to keep us from becoming "rough" as is found in bitterness, cynicism and rebellion.

When I attended our 48th High School Reunion, I was surprised many classmates didn't attend. Some of them stated they felt they had been slighted while in school and could not attend having had bad experiences with teachers and fellow students who did not value them. How sad to have kept this ill feeling for forty-eight (48) years. Many of us have had broken relationships but, with God's love and care, we are mended. We must not harbor these feelings for they cause bitterness. How many happy hours or joyful celebrations must we miss because of this bitterness? We must pray for wholeness.

THE RABBIT FOOT SHOW

It was the middle of May 1943, Aunt Idea and Miss Shug were busy getting their front rooms ready for roomers. From Batts to the West End, and Zion Hill to Rising Sun, posters were hung on every post or tree. From Love Station to Rabbit Ridge, people were talking. They asked, *"What is it? Where are they coming from? And, how long will they stay?"* The mystery added to the excitement. The Rabbit Foot Show was coming to Hernando, Mississippi! Lonnie Mae and I, both ten years old, wondered would it be a magic show? We knew having a rabbit foot was like finding a four-leaf clover. It meant you would have good luck or your hearts' desire.

There were no accommodations for blacks during this time and when they traveled, they stayed with relatives or in the homes of teachers, preachers or business owners. All of those in the revue were strangers, they would need rooms. We didn't know exactly what revue meant, but we knew it was not a religious experience as the preachers were preaching *"Dooms day"* and how the show would farther lead us down the pathway of sin and destruction. This added to the thrill, curiosity and anticipation.

Two weeks earlier, two tall, dapper, young men had come to town. They roomed with Miss Milly, the owner of a cafe on the West End. They were busy working out the details with different people. We heard some of the cast members were from New York, a blues singer was from the Delta area and a dancer had a peg leg. I wondered what a peg leg was.

The show would provide jobs for young men as laborers to set up the tents, spread saw dust and place the chairs. Women would be needed as maids to iron the colorful costumes. Valley Red, the owner of the "honkytonk" cafe out on Bell Road, was expecting an increase in business. Although his place was located way out in the rural area, he knew some people would want to party and gamble after hours. The merchants were excited as people from as far as Coldwater and Senatobia would attend. The bootleggers stock piled moonshine and hard liquor. The whole town was abuzz with excitement.

Our entertainment was limited to family and church activities. Occasionally, musicians walked the roads singing and playing juice harps and guitars, for their own pleasure. Sometimes they would play a special request for pocket change.

Finally the big weekend arrived. There were two shows, Friday and Saturday night. Two red and white tents were on the lawn of Baptist Industrial College. The smaller tent was used for dressing rooms. The long, flat bed of a truck served as the stage. It ran the length of the tent and on left stage was a combo with drums, piano, saxophone, trumpet and bass players.

The small lights hanging from the poles cast an eerie glow. The smell of saw dust filled the air; small boys were selling funeral home fans for a nickel or dime. The smart people brought their own fans from home. There was much laughing, calling out to friends and trying to save seats. Everyone was there, young and old. I even saw Rev. Thomas walk through.

After a long, loud drum roll, out on stage came twelve dancers, dressed in scanty, rainbow colored dresses. They were dancing the can-can and for every kick, the audience went wild. The Rabbit Foot Show had come to Hernando. The combo with its strong rhythmic beat, had people dancing in the aisles. *Rufus and Bones*, the comedians, kept the audience laughing with slap stick comedy about money or the lack of money, and relationships between men and women. A *"peg legged"* man tapped danced. There was much singing of the blues, ballads and jazz. I remember a lady in a red dress singing *"Don't get around much anymore."* This is my song now as an 89 year old.

The Rabbit Foot Show was a fast-paced, traveling minstrel show in the rural south during the forties. It lifted the spirits and was the topic of conversation for many weeks. It gave me something to dream about: visiting big cities, making money by singing, dancing or playing the piano.

SUNDAY MORNING

As a child, I related noise and food smells to Sundays. The smell of chicken frying or the beating of steak, are my fond memories of Sundays. Mother never slept late, she was up every morning at the crack of dawn. For Sunday breakfast, she might kill a chicken by wringing its neck, dumping it in a pot of hot water to remove the feathers, cut up, wash, season, batter and fry. The odor of frying chicken would get us up without having to be called. Sometimes we would wake to the pounding noise of Daddy beating a beef steak. Mother would fry the steak with onions and make thick brown gravy. Chicken and steak were served with rice, biscuits and homemade jelly, jam or preserves. After a leisurely breakfast we got ready for Sunday school and Mother started cooking Sunday dinner. Sometimes the vegetables were cooked on Saturday (greens or string beans, potatoes salad or sweet potatoes). The meat for dinner was fried or baked chicken, roast with potatoes and carrots, and during the hunting season: coon, possum, rabbit and deer.

I also associated Sunday morning with my great uncles, Cottrell and Luke. Daddy worked every day, but only three or four hours on Sundays, limited to selling things or small jobs. Every Sunday morning, Uncle Cortrell, my paternal grandfather's brother, came to visit and sometimes have breakfast. He lived in a small room under his sister Inez's porch across the street from us. Aunt Inez lived in a large two story white house, located on a hill. This was the big house on that section of Hemlock. Our neighborhood was culturally diversified; mostly whites lived on Parkway, the main through fare and blacks on the side streets Houses were of all descriptions from shotgun to large two storied. Maids, houseboys, teachers, preachers and other business men lived in the same area.

Uncle Cortrell was said to have *"spells"*. Surprisingly, few witnessed them, so some of the family and some people in the neighborhood thought he was lazy. His frequent saying was, *"No need to grumble, when you have a pocket full of crumbs."* We were not allowed in his room, but we peeked in and saw a cot, trunk and chair: all his furnishing. He showed us how to make string animals and told stories about family members who tried to be so *"uppity"*, but he knew the dirt on them. He frequently mentioned his sister Agnes, who had spells and was burned in a fire when they were children. This was a traumatic and frightening experience for him. He was always smiling, idolizing his sister Inez. He taught me to shoot marbles and I had a special feeling for him, for his child-like ways and winsome smile made him one of us. Everyone in the neighborhood knew him. He ran errands for the older people to earn pocket change. Sometimes he rode with Daddy on the truck, especially when he sold watermelons. He liked to yell, *"Watermelon man! Get your ripe melons here! Watermelon man!"*

I met Uncle Luke, my maternal grandfather's brother, when we moved to 84 West Trigg. This was after my parents' divorce, a difficult time for me. Our routine changed, no more big breakfasts, but Uncle Luke became a constant. He visited us every Sunday morning. He was an old man when I met him: dark and tall with stooped shoulders, and thick gray hair. He was always laughing and telling jokes, his favorite expression was *"first rate"*. Nothing could keep or get him down as he was *first rate*. It was said that he had been called to preach, but denied the call. While preaching about Zachariah, he forgot Zachariah's name. He said, *"And God told…and God told…"* after repeating this four or five times, he said, *"and God told… that man to come down out of that tree."* Uncle Luke liked whiskey and was never without his bottle. For years he worked on a river boat, three to four months away, and then one to two months ashore. He thought he was an embarrassment to his family and stayed away for months at a time. He married a second time at the age of sixty-two (62) to Miss Lillie, who owned her home and was a faithful member of the Church of God in Christ. Uncle Luke could drink in the house, but could not have his friends or drinking buddies visit. He laughingly said, *"I rarely stay in the house. Lillie's always begging me to stay home."*

Uncle Luke was an early riser and was our clock on Sunday mornings. He and I would listen to WDIA, discussed the preaching, church music and singing, especially the Wings Over Jordan Choir. We usually did this before I got ready for Sunday school.

I think of these uncles and their frequent sayings: *"Jesus never let us go hungry."* and *"He supplies all my needs."* *"Why complain?"* or *"I may not have as much as some people, but I have sufficient for this day."* *"I often think of Jesus feeding over 5,000 and having crumbs left"*. *"Why worry or grumble when I have all I need in my pocket?"* and *"Take these crumbs and make a dish."*

So, I learned to make something from whatever is on hand, for there is no need to grumble for I am **first rate** with a pocket full of crumbs.

FRESH YEARS

The night of our high school graduation, Bill walked me home from Mississippi and Walker Streets to West Trigg and Kansas Streets. We had our first talk. It was during the summer of 1950 that we began dating. We talked of our plans for the future. I told him my desire to see the world and what I expected of marriage. During 1953, Bill said I persuaded him to marry. He wanted to wait until he was financially secure and could show me the world. It was during that summer he rode his bike to ask Daddy for my hand in marriage. Surprisingly, Daddy said *"Yes"*. Bill arrived in D.C. the Thursday before the Labor Day weekend. Annie Belle's boyfriend had a car and took Bill to apply for the license in Maryland.

Bill met the Director of Male Dormitories at Howard University. Bill was approved and would be staying in Slowe Hall. The Director told Bill of a couple who wanted someone to *"House sit"* while they were on vacation. We married in Rockville, Maryland on September 4, 1953. We spent our two week "Honeymoon" in the couple's lovely three bedroom, split level home, at no cost. God always supplies our needs.

It was our last year of school, so he returned to Nashville. We started living together after he graduated from Tennessee State University, the last of May, 1954. We rented a room with Willie and Eula Mae Walker at 22 Bryant Street, N.E., about two blocks from Freedmen's and Howard University. Bill worked selling window fans and in construction. We returned to Memphis in late August, after I graduated.

PART II

LIVING AND BLESSED

1947-1956

If it had not been for the Lord on my side,

where would I be? Where would I be?

MARRIAGE

I was assigned to care for Ms. Seymore, the Assistant Nursing Director. She had gall bladder surgery. I was anxious and scared, but decided the care was no different, just given in a private room, and all of my time would be spent with Ms. Seymore. Ms. Seymore was very encouraging and advised me to enroll at Catholic University, as my senior project: teaching prenatal patients, was excellent. She would have told me not to marry, but I did not ask permission, but rather informed them that I was getting married in September. Mrs. Seymore's life was centered on nursing, as she never married. I thanked her for her kind words, but I would spend time with my husband, as I wanted a family more than a career.

I told Ms. Seymore how much I admired her. We developed a close and meaningful relationship. She gave me a beautiful gold perpetual calendar as a graduation gift. She also recommended that my extended time be reduced to one week.

Bill graduated from A&I University Tennessee State in May 1954 and I would stay in D.C. until I graduated in August. I went looking for a room to rent. I found two ads in the paper. The first was located on G Street, N.W. The house was a two story attached stucco with a nice front porch. I rang the bell and an elderly white woman answered. I said, *"I'm inquiring about the room for rent."* She looked at me with unbelieving eyes and said, *"We may have to go to school with you but, we will never live with you!"* She then slammed the door in my face. The **Brown vs Schoolboard** decision was on every one's mind.

The second house was similar except not attached and located on Bryant Street, N.E. Mrs. Eula Mae Walker answered the door, and she spoke with the distinct accent of the South Carolina Islanders. Mrs. Walker was a tall, stately woman. She lived in D.C. for twenty-five (25) years. She was a hardworking, industrious woman, with an innate ability to manage. Mr. Walker was from Maryland, they had been married for seven (7) years. He was a harsh, belligerent man, who thought he knew everything.

The house had a large living and dining rooms which the Walkers' used as their apartment. There were two (2) bedrooms and a bathroom upstairs. In the basement there was one large room, a wash room a large open area and bathroom. All total, there were nine (9) people in the house: The Walkers, two married couples and three men in the basement. The three men were from South Carolina and new to D.C. Mrs. Walker was very organized and had written instructions posted in the kitchen, with duties on 'when, who and how' to clean the stove, the refrigerator, the bathrooms, the dining room and the enclosed back porch.

Bill went to work selling window fans. Washington, D.C. seemed hotter than Memphis, Tennessee to us. There seemed to be no breezes stirring anywhere; and, heat waves were coming from the asphalt. We were sure Bill would do well selling fans at the price of $29.99, plus he would make $5.00 for each fan he sold. Bill did not have the most dynamic approach or confidence in the product, but he came home every night elated over the number sold. The first week he sold thirty (30). He was paid $55.00 (fifty-five dollars). The manager said most of the clients canceled or were not qualified. Each week the cancellations increased until Bill was paid only $10.00 (ten dollars) as his weekly pay. Many clients denied cancelling their orders. The manager collected the $5.00 (five dollars) per fan.

The ANA was having a reception for student nurses at a big hotel. I had a black A-line dress with a scalloped neckline in the lay-a-way. It took all of my little money to get it out. Sometimes when we paid our rent, we had nothing left. Some of my classmates brought food over to cook, saying they wanted a home-cooked meal. This gave us food for a week. We were glad to eat their leftovers.

Bill went to work with Mr. Walker to do construction work. A huge stone fell on the big toe of each of Bill's feet. He couldn't afford to miss work to seek medical care. Bill continues to have problems with irregular growth of the toe nails, including after he had them surgically removed.

Many of the girls and their boyfriends would bring over beer and drinks. We would sit on the porch and listen to music. I remember Alice from California exclaiming about some new records. The artists were Muddy Waters and Howlin' Wolf. I told them that we have people walking on Beale Street in Memphis and on the West End in Hernando that would be picking and singing just like them. Our talks would always return to segregation and injustice. We decided that we would work to change the conditions of the world.

So we made it until August. Soon it was graduation day! We got to meet many of our friends' families.

MY IMPETUOUS DECISION

We lived with Bill's Mama Sammie and her husband, Aaron James, on Simpson Street. I was studying for my state boards and Bill was awaiting his military orders. We left in October, Bill to Wright Patterson Air Force base in Fairborne, Ohio and I went to Washington, D.C. to take state boards. Bill was to attend Installation Engineering School, training as an Air Installation Officer. I returned to Memphis to find a letter from Bill stating how much he missed me and wished I was there. Impetuously, I called the train station, got the price of the ticket, and the time of departure of the next train. I didn't unpack, but asked Mr. Bunt to take me to Grand Central Station.

I had arrived at Union Station and would leave from Grand Central Station, which was a much larger station with a transfer in Chicago. After paying for my ticket, I had $7.00 left. I arrived in Dayton, Ohio at 5:30 P.M. on Saturday, with Bill's letter in my hand. I called Wright Patterson and said, *"May I speak to 2ⁿᵈ Lt. Willie L. Jones?"* The operator asked, *"What company or school?"* I answered, *"I don't know."* She said, *"Find something with his address and read it to me"*. I found the information requested and gave it to her. She called his battalion, but he was not there. She said, *"Maybe he is on his way to pick you up; did he know the time of your arrival?"* With a trembling voice, I replied, *"He doesn't know I'm coming. I wanted to surprise him and I'm scared. It's getting dark and I don't have much money."*

She assured me, *"We'll find him. Give me the phone number there and stay near the phone."* About 20 minutes later she called. *"We have located his Captain. They are trying to locate your husband. They think he is bowling."* I then found a newspaper on the seat and looked for a cheap room. My $7.00 was not enough for a taxi and a room. The operator called every 15 to 20 minutes.

At 8:30 p.m., Bill called. I was crying, and he asked, *"What are you doing here?"* I answered, *"You said you wished I was here. You didn't mean it?"* Bill reassured me and said, *"We are coming for you, but it takes 30 to 40 minutes."*

I will never forget the compassion of that operator or Bill's Captain. The Captain found quarters for us for that weekend. Fairborne, Ohio had few accommodations for African-Americans in the 50's. Throughout my life, God has placed people along the way to help me. I rest in the assurance that God is with me, even when things look dark.

MY STORY, TRANSFORMATION ON MY JOURNEY

I graduated from Hamilton High School in 1950. My first job was working for Mrs. Ann Pitchard, Registered Nurse, who worked in the doctors' office where my mother was a maid. Mrs. Pritchard was very kind and understanding. I was very anxious to please her. I was good at cleaning, but had problems ironing. I lasted two weeks, for after burning her good blouses she told me she'd help me find a job; and, she did in the office of Dr. Higley and Dr. Ray, orthopedic surgeons, as maid/assistant. I did light cleaning and helped the doctors. I enjoyed the patient contact. I admired the Baptist Student Nurses uniform. I thought they looked glamourous and decided I would become a nurse. I received a scholarship to Talladega College in Alabama. Since I did not know anyone that was a nurse, I thought this would be different. As I reflexed on my reasons to become a nurse, I am amazed at my shallow reasoning. Many people helped me to make this dream come true. I think God placed them in my path. As I prayed, I prayed for the reconciliation of my parents.

In 1950 there was not an accredited nursing school for African-Americans in Memphis, Tennessee. Daddy knew nothing about accreditation. He had heard of a young woman who had graduated from a school and couldn't take the state boards. She left Memphis and went to a school in Washington, D.C. He decided I should go to that school. The doctors encouraged me and had a big book listing colleges, medical and nursing schools. I found Freedmen's Hospital School of Nursing, the nursing school of Howard University. Mrs. Moore, the secretary, typed a letter requesting information and an application, signed and on the doctors' letterhead. I soon received a reply telling me to take an entrance exam. Mrs. Atwood my third grade teacher and later my Spanish instructor, gave me the test.

About the middle of August, I was notified I was accepted at Freedman's Hospital School of Nursing (Howard University). I think divine intervention was working for me. We rushed around trying to get ready. I had never been to a dentist and when I did, I found out I had three cavities. I needed glasses. We wondered how we could be ready in 6 (six) weeks. We went to A. Schwab on Beale Street and bought a large wardrobe trunk. This would hold more than what I owned. My sister, Inez, was in Hernando chopping cotton. She's going to buy me clothes with the money she made. Mother's brother, William gave me a watch with a second hand. Daddy made me a green swing back coat. I hate hand-made clothes. I packed it in the trunk first. Many of my uncles and aunts gave me five (5) to ten (10) dollars each. Daddy comes thru with Three Hundred and Fifty ($350.00) Dollars. I even received a donation from the church. I finally had Five Hundred ($500.00) Dollars. I'm ready to travel north to Washington, D.C.

I left in September 1951 from Union Station. I had never been more than twenty-five (25) miles from home, only to spend the night at my grandparents; never rode a train. Surprisingly, none of the relatives I knew had migrated north. So with fear and awe; they bid me farewell. Everyone offered advice. After visiting my grandparents, I am ready to leave. I dressed in a beige boxy suit. As I left home, my mother always said, *"Bless you, my child."* My mother had pinned Four Hundred and Eighty Dollars ($480.00) to my bra.

I kept looking around for I had heard of city slickers taking your money. I had lost twenty dollars ($20.00) in Sam's Grocery store and was considered careless with money. My mother and sister cautioned me about losing this money because we knew we could not replace it. I was scared, but thrilled; and, still patting my bra. Union station was a busy place, with much coming and going. I rode the Tennessean. It was clean and comfortable with separate cars for whites and colored. There was no dining room for us. I had a shoe box with fried chicken, bread, fruit and pound cake. I would only have to buy soda water. Mother kisses me and says, *"Remember your home training. Bless you, bless you, my child."* And I am off!

I found a seat next to a window, and put my shoe box and magazine down, and patted my breast. I looked around to see if anyone looks suspicious. A lady across the aisle smiled at me. She was a pleasant stout woman and she came over. We talked over into the night. She was from Holly Springs, Mississippi and worked for a Senator from Wisconsin. She has lived in Washington, D.C. for the past fifteen (15) years; and offered to help me adjust to D.C. This is how I met Mrs. Anniece Johnson who became a mother figure to me while I was in Washington, D.C.

When we arrived in Washington, she took me to the lower level, helped me to retrieve my trunk and hailed a cab. She went to the school with me. She indeed was like a second mother to me. I could go to her home for a good meal. She worked as a cook and I learned to eat different types of food from Ms. Anniece. This was the beginning of a long friendship. She told me how people from different areas lived. I was becoming educated. I have learned something from so many.

There are three women who were present in my life as I began my spiritual journey. Although I didn't know it at the time, they were a blessing to me and were making a way for my spiritual growth. In D.C., I could hear my mother talking to me all the time, saying, *"Be not afraid, God will take care of you." "God will take care of you." "Learn to lean on the Lord." "He'll make a way, somehow!"'* That was my first experience of wondering: *"What am I doing here?"* I met students from all over the United States, and many from Africa.

WHAT AM I DOING HERE?

Howard University (Freedmen hospital) was established in 1867 and is one of the top colleges for blacks. Among its' graduates are many top professionals, outstanding businessmen and politicians. The students were mostly from middle and upper middle class families, from every state and many African countries. It is located over eight hundred miles from Memphis, TN. The farthest I had traveled was to my grandparents in Hernando twenty or thirty miles. I asked, *"What am I doing here?"*

My mind flashes back; I am twelve years old and at mid-term was promoted from the sixth to seventh grade. Included in this all girl class were girls aged thirteen to sixteen. I was socially and physically immature. I was thrilled but frightened and looked forward to the move. I was met with sarcastic remarks, jeers and derisive laughter when I gave an incorrect answer. The things I didn't know were blown up or magnified.

My parents were having marital problems and in the spring they separated. Mother said she was leaving because daddy wanted another woman and he would not let us go with her. I was to be strong and take care of my sister. I was embarrassed over their separation and refused to answer any questions. This act (separation) was rare at this time. Somehow I felt responsible. I became quiet and shy, which was conceived as aloofness or snobbish.

In the seventh grade I had a class in sex education: the favorite subjects were boys and sex. When the teacher left the room, someone would get up and give a lecture on their sexual prowess. There was disagreement, even fighting over what boy liked what girl. Janey Sue was frequently taunted. Once Mary Alice said to her, *"I hear you are doing it with Robert all the time"*. The classmates all exclaimed, *"Oh!"* Janey Sue leaped up and put her hands on her hip and said, *"Yes, doing it is good if you know how to do it."* I wondered… and asked myself, *"How do you know… You know how to do it?"* This was the first time I asked the question,

"What am I doing here?"

MENTORS

Mrs. Anniece Johnson, my cultural mentor

Ms. Johnson taught me many social necessities, including how to set a table, how to present yourself and how to act at different activities. She worked for a Senator from Wisconsin for many years and was very knowledgeable of many high political activities.

I met Ms. Anniece on the train going to Washington, D.C. She was like a mother to me. I spent many weekends at her house. She helped me adapt to big city life. She even taught me how to order different types of food and the similarities of blacks and whites. I think the greatest thing she instilled in me was the assurance that I was special.

Ms. Minnie Robinson, my church mentor

I met Minnie Robinson in 1957 when we joined Parkway Garden Presbyterian Church. She was a young woman in her 40's. I was impressed with her knowledge of the Bible and the Presbyterian Church Polity; her activities helped me with my spiritual growth. I strived to be like Minnie in the church. I became a Sunday school teacher, played the piano at the morning services, President of the women at the church, and finally I became an Elder. I was able to get Minnie to tell her story.

Minnie Bragg Robinson was born in the Collierville, Tennessee area, about twenty miles from Memphis. Her father was a quiet man, who worked from sun up to sun down as a farmer to produce the nine (9) bales of cotton needed for rent, and the fifteen (15) to twenty (20) bales for the upkeep of the family. Her mother, the strong force of the family was not afraid of the *"powers that be"* and made feisty remarks and independent decisions. Minnie was the second youngest and the baby girl of the seven children. She was a puny, sickly baby, and had pneumonia at age five: a debilitating illness for a sickly child. Because of this illness she was pampered and did not have to work in the field as her brothers and sisters.

Minnie was nick-named Tinny. She remembers the joy of Saturdays with her parents, shopping for material to make dresses and visiting neighbors. She liked to ride horses, fish and hunt birds. She thinks of the fun of *"mudding"*, where her brothers took a hoe to a small pond, stirred up the bottom, jumped in and caught the fish as they came to the top.

At age seven, she started school when her mother thought her strong enough to walk the long distance. She was a quiet, studious and was considered smart. As a teenager, she was no longer sickly. Collierville Colored School went to the tenth grade, and a big event was the graduation exercise. Minnie's mother encouraged her children to finish high school, sending them to Booker T. Washington in Memphis or Woodstock, Tennessee. Minnie chose Woodstock Training School. The Negro high schools in Shelby County were E. D. Geeter and Woodstock.

Woodstock was about thirty miles from Collierville. It was a community within itself: the complex consisted of a large gray building with classrooms that were connected to the auditorium/gym; a shop and home economics building; a home for the principal and two dormitories. The girl's dormitory included the cafeteria; the first floor was occupied by the matrons and some teachers. The second floor held junior students and the third floor was for senior students. There were one hundred and fifty students in primer to eighth grade; and two hundred in grades nine (9) to twelve (12) and twenty (20) to twenty-five (25) teachers. Many teachers lived in the community and walked to school.

Minnie worked in the kitchen and washed and ironed clothes for the coach to help pay her tuition. She played basketball. The team was a drawing force in the community and the recipient of many awards. Many tournament games were held in Church Street Park auditorium on Beale Street. The large building was built by Robert Church, a wealthy Negro who bought some of the first bonds to help Memphis after the great Yellow Fever epidemic.

Minnie had opportunities to travel to many towns in Tennessee and Alabama for regional tournaments. As a star, she remembers the crowd yelling, *"Go Tinny Bragg! Go!"*

After graduation she returned to Collierville and worked for the National Youth Association, a married a man from a prominent Mississippi family; they moved to Memphis. After many separations, she moved in with her sister. Her mother took her two year old daughter to Collierville. Minnie worked many different jobs, finally working in the dietary department at Kennedy General Veteran Administration (VA) Hospital, where she met Sherman Robinson. She saved her money to attend Henderson Business College. After graduating she married Sherman and worked at the Memphis World, a Negro newspaper, located on Beale Street. After working eight (8) years at the newspaper she left there and worked twenty-eight (28) years at Manassas High School as secretary/treasurer.

Ms. Frankie Bodden, my nurse mentor

When I started working at the Memphis VA Hospital in 1957, there were only two (2) African-American registered nurses (RN) employed there, Frankie Bodden and Leontine Lucas. Frankie was the first African-American on the staff and Lucas transferred from a VA

Hospital in North Carolina. Frankie went out of her way to make me feel a part of the staff by including me at lunchtime and advising/guiding me on who were the people to avoid. There had been many African-American nurses who had applied to work at the VA, but they didn't get pass the orientation. I made it pass the orientation and became the third (3rd) African-American RN on staff.

Frankie and I became close friends through the years as we traveled with our husbands. Frankie and I would attend the symphony, various musicals and the theater. Frankie helped me to become secure in my ability to work in non-friendly situations.

This is Frankie's story: Frankie Bodden was born in Memphis, Tennessee and the oldest girl of nine (9) children. Her father, a quiet man was complemented with her feisty outgoing mother. He worked for the railroad and did odd jobs to support the family. The family attended Friendship Baptist Church. Frankie attended Memphis city schools, graduating from Manassas High. She had a brother who died in infancy. She remembers when a public health nurse, Mrs. Taylor, came to see her grandmother who lived with them. She had a slow healing ulcer on her leg.

As a young person, Frankie worked as a babysitter making $1.00 an hour and as a cook (using a cookbook), and at the YWCA. She wanted a different way of life and heard you could go to Grady Nursing School in Atlanta, Georgia, if your parents would give you $5.00 a month.

Grady Hospital, was a county teaching hospital, segregated by a tunnel into white and black hospitals. It was hard to get in and even harder to remain. Frankie went to Atlanta, took and passed the entrance examination. Students were sent home for the least infractions, but she was determined to remain at the school. During the probation period, the first six months, students lived in a large open dormitory room with 25-30 students. The instructors were mostly white, and she remembers a student being called to the carpet for referring to a black instructor as Mrs. After probation the students stuck together. They even went on strikes because different foods were served to blacks, and a doctor slapped a nurse. They did not return to class until the doctor resigned.

Patients were all in wards and were given good care. The students worked a split shift with a very strict regime. World War II caused a great demand for nurses, although many nurses and students left nursing to work in factories for the increased pay. The Bolton Act was developed to retain nurses pay for the training of nurses who signed up to remain in nursing careers for a designated number of years. The nurses were called cadet nurses and Cadet Frankie Holliday graduated in 1944. Frankie has fond memories of Grady: the parties in the dorm rooms, the USO, Peach Street Baptist Church and ladies from the YWCA. Three students were assigned to a YWCA representative, who took them to social functions. She laughed as she remembered eating chocolate mousse and other delicacies.

After graduation she worked in Jacksonville, Florida, Chicago, Illinois and Ann Arbor, Michigan where she attended the University of Michigan. She returned to Memphis and worked at the Health Department and for Metropolitan Insurance Company's nursing service. She was the first instructor for the Practical Nursing program, started by the Board of Education at Booker T. Washington High School. She could not go with her students for their clinical training at John Gaston Hospital. She applied at the Veterans Administration Hospital and was told she needed experience. She worked at John Gaston Hospital for one year and reapplied at the Veterans Administration Hospital and became the first black registered nurse. The patients were segregated, but she worked with both. She developed friendships with some of the nurses who were pleasant and helpful.

She continued her education at the University of Tennessee, Memphis State and Lemoyne-Owen College. During those early years she took all new black nurses to lunch and had informal 'get-togethers' each month at her home. Her quiet reassuring manner, teaching method and encouragement enabled many to remain at the VA.

Frankie knew Mrs. Little from the neighborhood was and thrilled when Mrs. Little invited her to attend a registered nurses meeting. She liked the people and the activities. The women were very professional, had a close relationship with black doctors and other professionals. She learned from the older nurses, organizing, planning programs and rules of order. The groups' teas, fashion shows and concerts attracted professional people. Their yearly trips, cultural events that members and friends could "lay-a-way" were well attended and a service to the community. She has served as president, chair of many committees and for many years treasurer of the club.

Frankie and her husband Ira, a renowned businessman and instructor, traveled extensively to Europe, Africa, Egypt and South Africa. She has helped financially and exposed her nieces and nephews and now great-nieces to cultural events. She's a lifetime member of Friendship Baptist Church where she is an assistant Sunday school teacher. She was a lifetime member of the NAACP and charter member Chi Eta Psi, Beta Chapter and Una Vocal Social Club. She likes the theater, symphony, jazz, swimming, socializing with her friends and visiting the sick.

THE REGISTERED NURSES' CLUB, INC.

The registered nurses' club is an outgrowth of the National Association of Colored Graduate Nurses. The NACGN was informally organized August 25, 1908 and formally organized in Memphis on April 2, 1924. For forty-two (42) years the NACGN functioned as did the American Nurses Association to improve and uphold the standards of nursing. Prior to 1951, nursing was represented by six national organizations. In May, 1950, a new structure was voted in with two national organizations known as the American Nurses Association and the Nursing League of America. The NACGN was dissolved January 26, 1951, as full integration of Negro nurses into the profession and its organization was its goal.

Minorities that integrate often lose their identity, forget who they are, and often lose their way. Because of these fears, the local chapter of the NACGN became a social club (RNC) in 1950, to develop cohesiveness, through support and fellowship, with emphasis and focus on educational, civic, social and community services.

THEY STOOD

For seventy five years of service,
The Registered Nurses Club celebrates
its members we declare are meritorious
Young, gifted and black, they came
From the north and south of Memphis…
Small towns of Tennessee, Mississippi and Arkansas.
THEY STOOD
Endured the hardships, working from dawn to dust,
In small clinics and hospitals, mostly owned by blacks,
With few amenities or modern equipment.
THEY STOOD
Valiant, vigorous and with valor Worked and
trained in hospital such as
Jane Terrell, Collin Chapel, Mercy and Royal Circle.
THEY STOOD
These early pioneers of the colored graduate association
Hatti Q. Avery, Aline Vance, Therese Perkins, Bessie Oakley,
Mary Robinson, Nettye Reaves, Eva Mebane, Fenton Little,
Alberta Lee, Nazerine Clarke, Eva Cartman Martin,
Lillie McGuire and Vigil Bynum. With effortless energy,
They were our "elite vital"
THEY STOOD
Never complaining of the slights and injustices they received, these
navigators worked and negotiated for inclusion In the American
Nurses Association. Stressing the importance of going the last mile.
They knew they must be better than others.
THEY STOOD
Tall, tan and terrific, black, bold and beautiful
Frankie Bodden, Bernice Freeman, Norris Grandberry,
Ruby Hines, Maurice Tate, Cornelia Tillman, Lillian
Thompson, Eugenia Smith, Doris Walker and Selena Watson
McClellan. These women have tirelessly woven a tapestry

of Perseverance, sisterly love and dedication.
Yea, often referred to as maid, aide, practical nurse
and/or girl. They never lost their nerve.
Working in different fields; hospitals, public health,
teaching, Doctor's offices and clinics.
Calm, cool and collected.
THEY STOOD
With faith for the future and for fellowship.
They became a social club, the RN Club,
For they feared loss of identity in a larger group.
With fervor and fun, fearlessly encouraged each other, traveled
together, presented young artists in concert and gave scholarships.
THEY STOOD
Illuminating the way for us to tread.
The first at many institutions, they left an impression wherever
they worked. Strong, Knowledgeable and Sincere
THEY STOOD.
Venerable, Veracious and Vigilant
These sisters of our vocation Teaching, nurturing
with care and compassion.
THEY STOOD
Ever faithful, walking the extra mile. These pioneers excelled.
From their lives and history we glean
Ethics, education, example and esteem for
THEY STOOD.

PART III

LIVING AND BLESSED

1957-1976

TRAVELING

1975 AFRICA
IMAGES OF HOME

I visited Africa in 1975. As a member of a team from the Presbyterian Church USA, we visited the mission fields. Our first stop was Senegal, and I was awed with the beautiful, colorful dresses of the women. Silenced with the sight of the place where slaves were held awaiting ships to sail to America. Impressed with the strength and stamina of those (my ancestors) who survived. Visited Cameroon, Ghana, Zaire, Nigeria and Kenya and I was overwhelmed with the hospitality and warmth of the people. I was surprised to see such large, crowded cities with people of many shades of blackness, Europeans and Arabs. I was fascinated with the stalls/shops lining the streets of old towns. I saw families, mothers, fathers and children all working out of the small shops. I thought of my grandfather who stressed work/sell whatever you can. Here was my beginning.

In parts of Africa, the greeting is *"Moya, have you eaten?"* With death and famine ever present this is a real problem. Many of the native fruits and vegetables are costly due to transportation. The land is drying up and droughts are frequent. Tribal wars added to the destruction.

The modern aspect of the cities, similar to western cities, was a surprise. There were skyscrapers, beautiful shops with western attire, designer fashions. Beautiful black women dressed in the latest and highly contour and the beautiful silk, gold threaded materials of native wear. The large spacious homes of the old genteel were impressive. I met a woman in her late forties (40's) or early fifties (50s) who was a world traveler. She had visited the USA, China, Russia and Europe in the 1930's. Her home was a large white Mediterranean style bungalow, enclosed in a large fenced yard with a gatekeeper. Her father was a chief in their village. How wonderful to know Africans who were well read and cultured. This was not the image that was projected through my readings and movies. I was acutely made aware of Africa, as a continent on this trip.

I was awed at black pilots, bankers, and other government workers, this was my first experience of seeing blacks run everything. Oh, what a wonderful sensation. I was overcome when I went inside a small round hut as I visited in the *"bush"*. Sleeping mats hung on the wall, the ground clear of all grass, vegetables hanging from the roof and fruits drying on the roofs. The village was composed of ten to twelve small huts in a circle. In the center of the compound, was a large tent like hut with the sides open, no walls, with a big chair for the tribal chief. Off to the side was an open area for cooking. I was impressed with the orderliness of the area. This image brought back to mind the Hawaiian or Polynesian people. How similar we all are. Some of our stories are similar in many cultures.

This image of home tells me our first home is spiritual. Our ancestors knew (God) the spirit was always present and before undertaking any task, they asked for guidance. God was present in the (wind, waves, fire, sun and moon). In this home was a place for everything, no clutter of holding on to material things. So should we free our lives for things that have no meaning, whether at home or in our churches: we must keep God present in all of our activities. We must have a place for everything (order). Many times we hold on to things we can't or never will use. We must rid ourselves of relationships that smother us, friends who add clutter to our lives with gossip, innuendos, rumors and negative thoughts. We must have order and know who's in charge. Some of our problems stem from not knowing this. With God at the center of our lives, guiding and directing us. The person who can best perform a task should be in charge of the task or activity, with God as the center of his or her live.

We visited homes of the middle class who had western style modern ranch houses with dish washers, washer and dryers, televisions and etc. In the home I visited, the young woman was a social worker and her husband a lawyer. These young professional women were concerned with child care, education of children and tribal tradition. Many of the same problems we as blacks face in America especially, how to keep focused on our culture.

1995 Israel
THE HOLY LAND TRIP

"How great is the Lord! How much we should praise him. He lives upon Mount Zion in Jerusalem. What a glorious sight! See Mount Zion rising north of the city high above the plains for all to see—Mount Zion Joy of all the earth, the residence of the great king."

A varied group of believers went to the Holy land with Pastor H. O. Kneeland of Union Valley Baptist Church. It was truly a *"trip of a lifetime"*. The group: Baptist, Methodist, Presbyterian and COGIC were met in Detroit and London by a white group of fellowship Baptists.

Via air conditioned bus we started our sightseeing with a visit to Caesarea, where we were amazed at the ruins of a theatre built by Herod the great. The acoustics there were outstanding in this open air theatre. Our guide had asked Willie "Bill" Jones to sing the day before because of his deep voice. He sang *"Deep River"* and received a standing ovation from the tourist from around the world. We visited Bethlehem, the birth place of Jesus and Nazareth, his hometown. The trip to the garden of Gethsesmane and Golgotha made Jesus' life real and scripture more spiritual and meaningful. Some members and Pastor Kneeland were baptized in the Jordan River.

A worship service in the garden of Gethsemane, crossing the Sea of Galilee in a motorboat which stopped in the middle near the site where Jesus preached to the multitudes was a very meaningful experiences. Many floated or waded in the Dead Sea, the feel (oily) and odor (medicinal) will be remembered. Some left written prayers at the Wailing Wall.

The beautiful scenery from the green farmland of Israel to the stark mountains and desert of Judah were inspiring. The Bedouins (nomadic people) and sheep grazing on the mountains were a beautiful pastoral scene. The food especially the breakfast buffet of Israel with olives, pickles, tomatoes, cucumbers, various fish, cheeses, boiled eggs and a variety of breads and the "fast food" of Palestine *"Fulafah"* will always be remembered. The group of conservatives, liberals, moderates with a Jewish guide and Moslem bus driver showed genuine concern and expressions of commonality on this pilgrim journey.

The journey culminated as we went up to Jerusalem. The sight of the beautiful white stoned walled city was a spiritual "Homecoming'. The combination of historical, cultural and artistic aspects was skillfully woven by the guide and for Christians was a meaningful spiritual experience. We felt the divine presence and all wish to experience again someday by a return pilgrimage to the Holy land.

2001 CUBA
TRAVEL STUDY SEMINAR

In the summer of 2001, I had the opportunity to visit Cuba with six members of Liberation Community Church in a travel study seminar. We arrived on a bright sunny day in Havana I was expecting the people to be hopeless, depressed living in a communist country. We were met at the airport by a group of women many afro members who prepared three meals a day and entertained us with stories of their lives.

The outgoing, friendly manner and the old model cars (30's, 40's and 50's) were shining and in good condition. It was exciting as the drivers yelled at us "Hello Americans"! The people we met in the church took their faith seriously. The church in Cuba plays a significant role in the society. Christianity had become more open since the arrival of the pope in 1997. We visited house churches in many neighborhoods. Many of these house churches' ministry was primarily served by children and youth.

As we ventured out in the rural areas the poverty was appalling. There were ministries that included agriculture, waste disposal and the production of bio-gas from farm animals' feces. This reminded me of my grandparents on the farm *"use what you have, make what you need."*

The group was entertained in the evenings with Cuban musicians and dancers. This gave us a break from some tense encounters with poverty. It highlighted the African and Spanish cultures that are dominant among Cubans. We experienced the love of both non-Christians and Christians in Cuba. Rev. Dr. J. Herbert Nelson stated, *"There is richness in the unity of the spirit of God's creation"*. The experience was summed up by Pastor Gail Nelson when she stated: *"The zeal and enthusiasm for living the faith as found in Cuba is something we need to learn"*.

Pastor J. Herbert Nelson's vision of utilizing the experience as a means of *'deeping'* the awareness of the Christian church and its relationship with the poor. It was designed to serve as a learning opportunity to teach the church members the role of the church and its relationship to the poor; and, to serve as a learning experience to implement ministries at Liberation Community Church. I became aware.

LIVE THE MOMENT

In the mid-seventies, my friend, Velma, had an opportunity to attend a workshop in Los Angeles, California. She decided to take her two boys and make it a grand vacation. They left home the last of May, with a map marked with all stops and planned sight-seeing trips. They visited caves in Texas and reviewed history lessons on the western states and Native Americans. At this time, Native Americans were called Indians. On the fourth day they arrived at the Painted Desert. She was excited over the beautiful colors of the desert. She described the formation of the rocks and stopped for the boys to get a good look.

Her boys were nonchalant, complained they were sleepy and tired, and would not get out of the car. Frustrated, she thought of the many extra hours and other sacrifices made to make the trip. She demanded in a loud shrill voice, *"Boys! Boys! Get out, get out and look at this Painted Desert".*

Many of us go through life without looking at God's beautiful world or enjoying the day. We are too concerned with getting to the next activity. There is beauty and joy all along our journey. We can become so involved with making a living, we forget to live. Sometimes I complain I haven't had time to write for two or three weeks. Then I realize it should not take the place of activities with family or friends.

Just as children, we start off excited, but get tired along the way. Our anticipation of the final destination is more important than the daily run. Many times we wait to live saying, *"When I marry, when the children finish school, etc.",* But God tells us to *"live the moment."*

BAE'S REFLECTIONS

I thank God for this blessed life I have lived, beginning with the people and mentors in my path. I have named many of them. I joined the RN club in 1957 and experienced traveling, opera experiences, concerts, symphonies, and other musicals. Many of these activities, I took my children to. We traveled to the Caribbean, Bermuda, and many major cities: east, west, north and south within the United States.

JOYS AND SORROWS

THE JOYS

CELEBRATE THE JOY!

May is the most beautiful month of the year, with it being not too hot nor too cold. There are flowers blooming everywhere, children singing, celebrations of Mother's Day and Memorial Day. The melody of *"Danced in the Morning"* is played frequently on television commercials. I first heard that song at Presbyterian Church USA General Assembly, in 1992, Milwaukee, Wisconsin.

CHORUS:
> *Dance then, wherever you maybe,*
> *I am the Lord of the dance said he,*
> *And I'll lead you all, wherever you may be,*
> *And I'll lead you all in the dance said he.*

In this month just after we celebrated his death and resurrection, I am reminded to celebrate the joy and dance. I am stirred and whirl around the room. On arising…nothing is as beautiful as the rising sun and the awakening of a new day, where we are to do His will—seek His word and glorify His name. All in between the rising and setting of the sun, we should celebrate the joy, the births, the deaths and the bearing of our crosses. Dance, wherever we may be, for He is the Lord of the dance says he. We dance in different ways, fast thumping, slow swaying, sometimes just waving the hands or head, but all to His glory. I dance in the joy of my family, children, grandchildren and friends.

JOY IS

A beautiful fall morning after a stormy night

JOY IS

A letter from an old friend.

JOY IS

A reasonable portion of health and strength.

JOY IS

The birth of my grandson!
My sixth grandson: Justin
Long hands, big feet and a loud cry.

WHAT JOY!

Sing a Song of Joy

Sing a Song of Joy on this beautiful spring morning.
The peace within my heart for I have given it over to God.
All the agony of the children's broken
Lives,
Joblessness and Despair,
I know that God is still here with me.
So I sing a song of joy,
What joy!
Mema! ___ Mema!
The little ones cried
With uplifted voices and bright shiny eyes
They bounce on me
Tim Tim __ the quiet one

Terrell ____ the terrific Tumbler
Aaron __ with the deep Jones voice!
What Joy!

WE PRAISE THEE

We praise thee, O God, for the rain that bringeth life to the plants,
Without you, I would be nothing.
All that I have and ever hope to be, I owe it all to thee!
I give my everything back to you,
I thank you for life—even in the midst of the storms—I rest assured,
You are here!
I have not lived as if I trust wholly in you.
My doubts and fears, my concern over my children.
Not going to the aid of others.
Waiting on others to do,
I confess, I don't show your love to all.
Help me, Lord!
I try to live as Jesus taught, but fall short.
Forgive me. Lord!
I thank you God for the rain…that aids and nurture.

BILL

Before I knew you as Bill,
    I knew you were the one;
    I loved you as Willie Lee.
    Listen to our story.

In 1945 at Hamilton school, in the 7th grade, I met a boy named Willie Lee Jones. I, along with seven (7) other children, was promoted at mid-term from seventh grade to the eighth grade. I knew most of the students from the community or neighborhood churches, but not Willie Lee.

The girls and boys were in different rooms. Hamilton was a small school and relationships soon developed among the forty (40) to fifty-five (55) students. My parents separated that year and I was distraught and very quiet. The boy's teased me about my thick, husky plaits.

After the divorce of my parents, my mother moved with Cousin Jane on Trigg Street. During that time, Daddy let us go live with Mother. She rented the house and Cousin Jane moved with Aunt Laura. We had a four (4) room bungalow, with an enclosed back porch. I stayed in shock most of my time on Trigg Street. I kept imaging being back on Hemlock Street. Daddy's money enabled him to hire a lawyer. My mother only received a $1000 settlement. Daddy put his property in one of his brothers' name, which he lived to regret.

FORTY YEARS

It's our 40th wedding Anniversary!! I can't believe the years have passed so swiftly! It seems like yesterday we were busy making plans on how our lives would be lived. All the plans and good intentions—where did they go? The children are grown, some good and some bad, nothing outstanding (just like their parents and grandparents before them) now we are reaching retirement. The Lord has been good to us. We still have good health, able to work and enjoy some of the finer things of life.

Saturday evening we went to Wanda Jackson's wedding at Parkway Gardens Church. It was beautiful with streamers from the sidewalk out front —candles and long netting on the pews except the last four. There was a large candelabra in the center and with two smaller ones on each side. The soloists were girls with beautiful voices. The wedding didn't start on time and each groomsman and bridesmaid walked down the aisle alone. The girls had a little rocking dance step. The wedding was over at 7:00 pm. Then we went outside for the ceremony of the doves where an evangelist took fifteen (15) to twenty (20) minutes expounding on the meaning of the doves in a Christian wedding. We left about twenty (20) minutes to 8:00 p.m. for the reception at the Airport Hilton. There was another ceremony, the introduction of the wedding party and AKA ritual and eating about 9:30 pm. How different from our marriage ceremony.

I'M BLESSED

For the fun, family, friends, fellowship and more,
For the omnipresence of God who guided and directed our way.
From a naïve twenty year old,
To a maturing sixty-five year old,
I thank God for this day, our **Forty-Fifth Anniversary.**
I'm blessed.

It's revealed in my continued love that reaches
Heights unknown.
From Rutha, Baby Mae, Honey, Bae, Mama and Mema.
Through travel, talk, and the theater, we found pleasure.
I praise God and thank Him:
For your encouragement, for my many hobbies and activities,
Which became all-consuming,
Our beautiful children: Billy, Linda and Timothy,
Our transformation through Christ who
Helped us in our disillusioned, dysfunctional lives.
Yes, Thank You, Lord.
I'm blessed

For our family, yours and mine, that melded into "Our" family.
For the clouds of witnesses that Protect us every day.
The memories of family and mutual friends with all the joy it brings.
For imperfections, deceit, and loss of trust that drew us closer to God,
Allowing me to find myself in volunteering.
To arrive victorious, valiant to verify our love, Eternal and Everlasting.
I'm blessed.
HAPPY ANNIVERSARY!!

THE BIG 70TH BIRTHDAY

Sitting in your big blue chair nodding,
Listening to jazz and watching TV,
It's alright, for now you have reached the big **70**.
You with nerves of steel,
As you sped through life,
In your Simca, Opel, Fiat, Falcon, Nova, Toyota and Nissan.
Cars supposedly made to last, But short-lived with you.
Always depending on the Everlasting One.
And ever mindful of your responsibility to God, family and church.
You ventured out to travel to places unknown,
And your nonconformist ideas
Many times caused you to stand alone.
For your tender loving care with
Buster and Mattie's daughter.
For forty-five years
I declare you meritorious.
We note the music you played in our lives,
Whether melodious or off key.
And your tolerance of our musical attempts;
On the drums, guitar, recorder flute, trumpet, piano and organ.
Yea, and learning to live with the dogs,
Andy, Andy II, Classy, Jeremiah and Queen.
Hair now silver, father of three and grandfather
Of eight, rest assured of our love,
For we thank God for your seventy years,
He has blessed you and
You passed the blessing on to us.
Praise God!

THE AGE OF 90

Bless the Lord, O My soul
And all that is within me.
Bless his Holy name!! For He has given Bill 90 years on this earth,
And 68 years to bless me as his wife.
Thank you, Lord.
Give us many more.
To glorify in your goodness,
For our children and grandchildren,
And to do your Holy will
To see the needy as holy,
And work to bring justice to the world.

THE TRANSFORMATION

(FROM DIS TO THAT)

I randomly chose a name from the list posted at the old Treadwell High School. I had finished the required training for the *"Each One-Teach One"* Program. I was excited to begin teaching someone to read and surprised to find so many young people did not know how to read. Charles Miller was the name I chose: a twenty-two (22) year old African-American, who lived in north Memphis. I was to call to set-up a time and place for our sessions.

I called the Rev. Grant, who would make all arrangements. He had met Charles at the Shelby County Correction Center and was helping to rehabilitate him. He found Charles a job as a janitor at Christ United Methodist Church. He was also encouraging him to learn to read. I agreed to meet Charles on Tuesdays and Thursdays, from 4:00 p.m. until 6:00 p.m. at the main library. I agreed that if Charles could not attend, he was to call me.

Tuesday I rush to the library, obtained a study room and waited for Charles. At 5:30 p.m., I decide, *'he's not coming'*. I call Rev. Grant; he's disappointed, but will try to have him there Thursday. I asked, *"Do you think it would help if I talk to Charles?* He had no phone or permanent address.

Thursday I obtained the study room and waited. At 4:30 p.m., a young man hesitantly enters the library. He's wearing blue jeans, a plaid shirt and a green scrub cap on his head. He has a rolled newspaper under his arm. I smiled and greeted Charles. He has a thick guttural sound that made it difficult to understand him. I tell him that I have children his age, where I worked and the joy I have found in reading. He keeps his head down and says, *"Dats what I wants to do—read, specially the Bible and newspaper"*.

Charles and his family moved to Memphis from a town in Arkansas when he was ten (10) years old. He was placed in the second grade. He was big and tall for his age and his family lived in different areas of North Memphis. He said the children always laughed at him and the teachers ignored him. Sometimes he would spend two years in a grade before he was promoted. At age seventeen and in the eighth grade, he quit school. Soon he was hanging out with boys on the corner, selling drugs, robbing and stealing. He was in and out of jail. That's where he met Rev. Grant and was impressed with the minister's knowledge of the bible. He now attends Rev. Grant's church.

Charles and I met each week, and I encouraged him to talk and helped with his enunciation. We also talked about impressions: such as how you stand, what you wear, and your general appearance. He told me that the carrying of the newspaper was his impression. He said, *"I want people to think I can read."* He rarely mentioned his family. He had lost contact with them and was not sure where they lived now. I encouraged him to locate his family.

It was a joy to see and hear the transformation of Charles. When our sessions began and Charles needed to cancel a meeting, the people at work would ask, *"Who is that person? We can't understand anything he is saying"*. He no longer wears a scrub cap; and he removed the greasy activator and cut his hair. He lived in a rooming house and studied every night. He couldn't believe that he was learning to read. He finished one book—two books-three books. In four months, he was reading at the fourth grade level. His goal is to read in Sunday school. He began to walk with his head held up high; and shoulders back with a smile on his face. He was beginning to read the newspaper with understanding.

During our eighth month of sessions, I encouraged Charles to work towards getting his G.E.D. He can read at the sixth grade level. He is a confident, congenial person, and now talks about issues and invites young people to his church. He met a young lady and invited her to the church. They are now dating. She has invited him to meet her family. I am so happy for him and I asked him to invite her to our sessions. He doesn't want her to know that he's just learning to read. Charles started to miss classes, and, after six weeks he finally called to cancel the sessions. He can't explain to his lady friend where he goes every Tuesday and Thursdays evening.

I think of Charles frequently. My meeting him reminds me of how God transforms us. We are new persons with a different walk and talk. Many times, we don't want to let others know that he is present in our lives.

CHURCH

I see God in the quietness of a church. I feel Him in the singing of old hymns and songs. The gospel hymn, *"Rock of Ages"* says to me that God is always near. This was Grandfather Alf's favorite song. I can hear my mother singing the gospel song, *"The Lord will make a Way Somehow"*, as she washed and cleaned. Daddy would sing, *"I'm so glad, trouble don't last always, O My Lord, What Shall I Do?"*

I remember the foot thumping, rhythmic acapella singing of the rural churches of my grandparents. Mother joined St. Jude Baptist Church when we moved on Hemlock Street. Many of the members were from Hernando and other small towns of northern Mississippi. The fervent prayers and soul filling songs still bring goose bumps and tears to my eyes. The preachers started off slowly, but gradually reached a crescendo ending when many members were shouting, throwing purses, and running up and down the aisles.

As a child, I attended St. Jude with my mother, Greenwood CME with Aunt Inez and East Trigg Baptist with Earnest and friends. At the age of 12, I went to the mourners' bench and on the third night, I made my declaration of faith and accepted Jesus Christ as my Lord and Savior. I was baptized and joined East Trigg Baptist Church. Dr. W.H. Brewster was the Pastor and a great preacher and teacher. He became famous for his song writing and poems.

Mother was very active in church and always joined a neighborhood church when we moved. She would sing in the choir and attend all worship services. Most Sundays, it was Sunday school, 11:00 a.m. worship services, 3:00 p.m. Special services, Baptist Training Union and Evening worship. My parents divorced when I was thirteen (13) years old, and the subsequent move to south Memphis was very traumatic. I joined Bloomfield Baptist Church on Kansas Street at Mother's insistence. Mother was very active as usual. I was angry and rebelled by not participating in church activities. I was sad by the changes in our lives. I missed visiting our grandparents every week and of course my father's presence. I was searching for the meaning of life and read the Bible extensively.

The many negative expressions of my father kept coming to mind. *He would say, "They only want money. The preachers and deacons are all having sex with the members."* I remember him mocking the preacher. He would grab his ear, rub his stomach, wipe his face and moan, saying: *"oh—shout, sho – out. Oh, sho -out—you"*. Daddy would insert any word: *(s.o.b., dogs, cats, mules, bastards, etc.)* He said the members never heard what was said; they were looking for an emotional high.

I was concerned with what I called the Jenkins curse, and wondered if it would fall on me. My uncles and my daddy were known womanizers. I didn't know of the girls actions, as they were very sheltered, and rarely dated. The men were considered good looking, self-assured, sometimes to the point of arrogance.

THE RETIREMENT PARTY

Yesterday, July 22, 1995 was the culmination of twenty-five years of service at the Memphis Shelby County Health Department. I was given a beautiful reception headed by Cynthia Chatman with assistance from the office of nursing, especially Carol Ballard, chief of nursing and Brenda Kinney, consultant.

The administration conference room was decorated with peach and light green balloons, in groups of threes, with gold ribbon and a large butterfly in front and all around the room. Three chairs were in front, under a banner that stated ***"Happy Trails to Rutha!"*** Next to the table in the corner was a table draped in white and loaded with gifts, a large plant, gold mums, red roses and beautiful bags and gift wrapped presents. The table was covered with beautiful white cloth and resplendent with a silver

A bowl of punch and trays were from Gloria Mercier, two large cakes, green and peach with butterflies gracing each end. In the center there was a floral arrangement sent from Linda and Greg, elevated on a bowl so the punch bowl and centerpiece were the same height. From the centerpiece on each side was a large porcelain butterfly and a gold streamer covered with laminated butterflies of all colors—meat trays of ham, turkey, meatballs, cheese, olives, fruits, vegetables and dip, mints and peanuts. There was plenty of everything. Friends and acquaintances from all floors came to wish me *Godspeed!*

A lovely program started with the kind words of Cynthia Chatman who praised me as a role model to my co-workers; a poem written by Marshell Brown was presented to me on a plaque; a flute rendition of *"You Light Up My Life"* by Naomie Spencer Gammon; and a solo by Jacqueline Rodgers, *"The Wind Beneath My Wings"*. I cried, for all of them were so sincere, and they had done so much to make my retirement party a beautiful occasion. I wonder why I never feel I'm worthy of the praise, and that what I've done is nothing. Dr. Kirkland read a citation from Mayor Rout of Shelby County and Ms. Madlock read a plaque of my contributions to the citizens and co-workers of Shelby County. MeDear, Bill, Bae, Edna, Vera, Frankie, Johnnie Riley, Pastor and Mrs. Cable, Sadie Williams, Peggy Conner, Nana, Papa and Margie were present. I received many nice gifts, all listed in a book, and $350.00 in monetary gifts. I left there at 4:15 p.m., with the back seat of my car full of balloons and my eyes full of tears. Another beginning.

ROCKING CHAIR

I received money from friends and co-workers as a retirement gift. Many heard me say, I would take the first year to do nothing but sit on my porch and rock. So, I used the money to buy two rocking chairs. One is on the front porch, it is unfinished, painted white but the paint can't hide its roughness. So it is with us. We are rough and unfinished. Coating or painting won't cover the stains or roughness. Often we try to cover with fine clothes, pretty houses, furs and luxury cars, etc. Yet, with these material things we still live in the gutter, having sex with multiple partners, cheating on husbands or wives and drinking excessively, to name a few.

As I sit in my chair, on the front porch and watch the sun rise, I am at peace. The rocking motion reminds me God sent us the Great Comforter, the Holy Spirit to guide and direct us. Whatever the problem, God can smooth out the roughness. The Spirit tells me to let go of my concern for my daughter who is in the midst of a marital conflict, my son who can't find a job and the other son who has such a nonchalant manner. I feel the high back and strong arm rest as I watch the squirrels scampering up the tree and the children playing. This gives me a secure feeling God is in control. He orders the new day, and I know he will care for me. What peace comes from this assurance? The firm seat and support for my arms and back remind me of God as our Father, who will provide all of our needs. Like the squirrel gathers and hides his nuts, God will show us how to prepare for the raining season.

The second chair is in our bedroom. It is smooth, varnished and stained a light beige color. A cushion in the seat and back denote comfort, for God gathers and comforts us, like a mother hen gathers her baby chickens. When we find Jesus Christ and turn our lives over to Him, our lives can be smooth. The sanding knocks off the rough places. Just as the chair is streaked with light and dark stains, so does Life have bright and dark moments. As I sit in this chair in the evening, when the sun goes down, to rock a grandchild to sleep, read the paper or listen to the news. I can always use this chair, no matter the weather. Its tall, firm ladder back reminds me I can always reach God and I'm sheltered in His love. The cane bottom firmness denotes God's faithfulness. He is always there, sharing everything, the good and the bad. He never leaves us.

My rocking chairs remind me of God. The peace that comes from Him, even in the midst of trials and tribulations, God is always there. He is faithful. So, I rock and reflect on how I can bring others to know Jesus Christ.

INEZ

How we take things for granted
Such as the presence of sisters.
I cannot remember when she was not there,
 My sister.
The pretty one, we called her fair child,
 My sister,
We slept together for seventeen years, mostly in a half iron bed,
I always tried to act unafraid to protect
 My sister

She decided to chop cotton, to send spending money,
While I was away in school.
She calmly went about her daily activities,
Working and rearing three boys.
 My sister.
Now she's able to relax, going to Hawaii
Our first time traveling together,
How wonderful—thank God for

My sister, Inez.

This was written May 1996. I was elated that Bae and I would travel together. This would be our first time traveling together. She and her husband, Emmet had planned and paid for the trip, but in June, he was diagnosed with lung cancer and was unable to go, yet encouraged her to go. He asked if I would travel with her, I immediately said "yes".

 It's amazing my sisters are both excellent caregivers, going the last mile… forgetting about self, Truly Christian.

MARGIE

Magnificent, majestic and malleable
Practices the gift of love,
My little sister of love, Margie.
Cheerful, quiet and calm
With an attitude that causes no harm
Opened her heart and arms to me
When I married her brother, Willie Lee,
My little sister, Margie
Was always there when you need her nursing skills,
in the family or community.
Oh, how I love and respect her.
Gladly I will go to bat for her.
Her life shines like a bright star!
My little sister, Margie.

I have been surrounded with love from many people. I know I'm blessed to have such in-laws.
I gained a sister when I married.

ALEXIS DENISE

We welcome you today all 1 pound and 9 ounces of you,
This beautiful summer day.
Come into a family where you are adored. Love so endearing, so divine
Greets you this blessed morn.
God in his merciful grace, Brings to us this day
A miracle child are you.
I pray you will be
Admired,
Loved,
Educated and energetic
Zealous in your love of God, family and church,
Intelligent with the ability to learn and respond from the experiences of your life.
Secure in the knowledge you are God's child and one of the Joneses.

LEAP FROG

DEDICATED TO MY GRANDCHILDREN

Trust in the Lord
As you approach each birthday, remember to leap
frog. Jump into whatever is before you!

L   is learning to listen to the word of God. Lean on the Lord.

E   is being enthusiastic. Seek education.

A   be active, physically and mentally.

P   is for prayer. Stay connected to God.

F   be a friend. Develop lasting friendships.

R   read the Bible. Be responsible.

O   be an optimist. Look for the good in everything.

G   be generous. Give to those in need.

Make a difference in your life.
Make a difference in at least one other life.

An Irish Blessing

May joy and peace surround you, contentment latch your door, and
Happiness be with you and bless you ever more.
May the road rise up to meet you.
May the wind always be at your back.
May the sunshine warm on your face and rain fall soft on your fields,
And until we meet again,
May God hold you in the palm of His Hand.

JOYS AND SORROWS

SORROWS

I MOURN

Woke to a beautiful morn, looked out at well-kept lawns
And large stately houses. Suburbia.
I mourn.
For the boarded up houses on Simpson Street,
For those who cannot escape and still call it home.
Took my grandson to a brand new elementary school.
It had all the latest equipment and materials.
Enthusiastic teachers and staff.
I mourn.
For inner city schools, dedicated teachers,
Worn out mentally and physically.
Poor working conditions, not enough or lack of latest equipment.
For the children who were up late,
Fighting heat, roaches or each other.
Parents who have no hope.

I mourn.

This was written in August 1995 while I was staying with my daughter, for the birth of her third child. I could not imagine or believe we would soon mourn for her and the boys—loss of house, cars, but most of all, for her losing her joy.

IZZIE

I met Izzie the summer of 1947. We were both fourteen (14) years old, lonely and day dreamers. She was tall and willowy with a light honey brown complexion, sandy hair, French braided or in a pompadour for dressy occasions. She had brown eyes and always had a warm smile. She had lived with her grandmother in Wilson, Arkansas until two years ago when her grandmother had a stroke and moved to Memphis with a daughter; and Izzie came to live with her mother, who had an addiction. They lived in an apartment complex with a room and a kitchen. The front steps led directly to the sidewalk. Many of the occupants were alcoholics: the women did day work and the men walked to Florida and Trigg where white men looked for laborers. The apartments were painted off-gray that was typical of the times. The children played on the long back porch and in the street. I envied them as we couldn't leave the yard.

Izzie was developing a full, shapely figure. Men and boys would make loud noise and lewd remarks as she walked by. Once Izzie went to cafes on Florida Street looking for her mother and found her drunk in a cafe. The men made lewd suggestive remarks. She no longer looks for her mother but sits by the window and waits for her to come home.

Once a month we walked to Main Street, from riverside. This was exciting to me for I had never gone up town. Izzie was a good swimmer and told how relaxing she felt in the water: she could bury her cares when swimming. We went to the big department stores admiring the pretty clothes, shoes and furniture. I remember trying on a hat in Gerber's' department store. The elderly saleswoman was very upset, and in a loud, shrill voice, screaming, *"You colored girls can't try on hats and y'all know it"*. We left the store with everyone looking at us. After a couple of hours we hurried home to listen to Stella Dallas on *Portia Faces Life*, on the radio.

I couldn't go to the apartment complex so, Izzie visited me. We sat on the front porch and made up stories on the people passing by or on the streetcar. We would be beautiful well dressed women with handsome husbands, going to big cities like Paris France and New York City. I would be a social worker and own a brick house; Izzie would be a model or hairdresser. We would be two beautiful, successful women.

Izzie and I liked the Brown brothers, Joseph and Alvin. We didn't know they probably looked down on us as their father was a railroad man. I told Joseph of my longing to return to Hemlock Street, where things were normal before the big divorce. One day Joseph went to Hemlock Street. He came back and told me, *"I don't know why you want to go back to*

Hemlock Street. You are living better here on Trigg." Izzie loved Alvin. They went to the movies every Sunday. I talked to Joseph on the street car, as I didn't receive company. Alvin went to Tennessee State College and his letters became infrequent. When he came home for Christmas, Izzie noticed he had changed. She was depending on him to take her out of the apartment complex; she never dreamed of doing it herself.

In the spring, Izzie was pregnant and Alvin was writing very infrequently. I was surprised mother let me continue our friendship as one of her saying was, *"Birds of a feather stick together".* She had a beautiful baby boy. At that time, girls didn't return to school after having a baby. Some families with money sent the girl out of the district or town.

I continued going to Hamilton high school. Mother scrapped up money for five rides a week. I rode the streetcar every morning and walked home every afternoon. I started dating in the eleventh grade. Izzie and I grew apart. She was busy with the baby and I with school.

The summer I graduated from high school Izzie was pregnant again: they say from a white man. I angrily confronted her for not working on our dreams and the audacity of going with a white man. I remember her blank look as if I wouldn't understand. *"White men give me money—our boys look down on me because of where I live. My family always lived this way".* We talked and talked but I could not convince her that she could change her situation.

I went away to nursing school. Our house burned down and mother went back to Hernando. My sister, Inez, moved back with Daddy on Hemlock Street. My letters to Izzie were returned, stating: *"not at this address".*

Three years later while home for the summer, I read in the paper that a young black woman drowned in the Mississippi river. It was Izzie! I wonder what I could have done to ease the pain and hopelessness she felt. I think of Izzie as the tide comes in and as it goes out.

BUSTER

January 1, 1993 was a cold gray day in Memphis. The visibility was at 30 feet and there were very few cars on the street. It's a perfect day to watch the super bowl football game. In his daughter Inez's front bedroom, daddy lies in a hospital bed. His body is racked with pain, unable to turn, wearing diapers. He drove up from Hernando two weeks ago with swollen hands and feet and he has grown progressively weaker and is now unable to bear any weight on his legs. He thrashes about with pain, gasping for breath, between moans, he yells, *"no work, no pay."* He is diagnosed with high blood pressure, diabetes and gout. His daughters are trying to keep him comfortable as they fear he is dying. I rented a hospital bed and a lifter and applied for equipment from the Veterans Administration.

I and my father had a love-hate relationship, as a child I did everything I thought daddy expected. I was a daddy's girl, and was told I looked like him. I tried to walk like him. Daddy told me *'I could do anything if I applied herself'* and I believed him. As a young woman, we had many confrontations, but now we accept each other's differences. He now goes about the community boasting of his first born, *"She will stand up to anyone".* I had come to grips with my love for him even though he has caused me much embarrassment with his rebellious ways and unorthodox actions.

Inez, the younger daughter works nights in a nursing home, rushes home to give her father good care. She is an excellent care giver. Apparently she has forgotten or wiped out memories of his demanding, cantankerous, controlling attitude.

Daddy has little faith in doctors and seeks medical assistance only at his daughters' persistence. He has treated himself by using his knowledge of herbs and home remedies. While in the army, he received electric shock; it's unknown why, but he says it was their means of controlling him. He was discharged with a medical discharge, but would not consent for examinations or medicine. His pension was denied, and at age seventy-seven, Inez's husband insisted he reapply. He did, was examined, reassessed and his pension started. He still refuses exams and checks himself out of the hospital against his doctors' advice.

He was constantly hitting the walls with his cane, screaming, *"I can't stay in this bed, it will sap my strength."* So, he was in and out of the bed. After two and a half weeks he was better and wanted to go to Hernando every other day, to check on his dogs, pay bills or take care of his business.

Buster talks a lot of the past and Inez thinks he is senile and needs to move in with her. Of course, he will not tolerate this idea. He has to drive his truck. He and Inez have an argument; he demands she give him his keys. Inez calls me and says, "Come get your Daddy!" "So, I take him to my house. He walks every two hours until he walks the length of the house. He gets his brother, Leroy, to get his truck and to take him to Hernando every other day. After two weeks, I come home to an empty house. Daddy (Buster) has gone back to Hernando. He had been driving from his house to the square every other day. He's glad to be home, back to visiting, selling vegetables and being his own boss. That's my Daddy!

A Pocket Full of Crumbs!

MICHAEL

When Michael was told he had a malignant tumor, we were all devastated… Not Bae's first born, Mattie's first grandchild and my first nephew. Especially at this time, where we stood around the bedside of Emmett Jr., his father, who was dying of cancer, and being kept alive on a respirator.

Michael, the strong one, the drum major, the one who was always laughing. Michael said, *"I'm strong, I'll walk again."* But in three weeks the cancer had spread to his spine and wrapped around the bones in his neck. This condition caused him severe pain and paralysis from the waist down.

I rushed to the hospital, I could sense his fear. He had never been sick. He was scared of doctors and hospitals. It was our job to reassure him that everything would be alright. As we waited on the doctor and x-ray report, we laughed together as we remembered the time when Michael was a two (2) year old and knocked down Me'Dear's screen. As a little boy, he was rambunctious and was moving around a lot in Me'Dear's room. Our famous words at that time were, *"Oh, don't worry, he can't do any harm"*. Well Michael fooled us that day. He knocked down the decorative screen-room divider. Now, sitting beside his bed, I told him, *"you are strong, you have been strong for forty-two years. Knock down these obstacles! Rely on God's grace."*

Like incandescent light…Love flowed from mother, brother, children, ex-wife, grandmothers, aunts, uncles, cousins, co-workers and friends. Their support showed God's love through their faces and actions. This faith helped us. For this was our support group. Praise the Lord!

The caring compassion of friends and hospital workers, from doctors, to housekeepers helped to broaden our support group. This affirmed my belief in the goodness and faithfulness of God and man.

Through it all, Michael's humor abounded. As we gathered in neuro- intensive care, the night of his surgery, we were torn with anguish, weeping inside, trying to present a calm reassuring front. My sister, Bae, said to Kenneth, his brother, *"Michael just had a little surgery to relieve the pain and hopefully to help him walk again"*. Michael said, *"What do you mean…a little surgery. I have been cut from my neck around to my spine, and you call that little"*? It broke the ice and tenseness as we all laughed at him; the real Michael is still here.

Michael was in and out of the hospital with chemo treatments, radiation therapy and blood transfusions. After three months we were told to, *"Keep him comfortable, it's a matter of time"*. Lord, please give me the strength to endure. He expressed anger over not being allowed to attend his father's funeral, and was sent home two days later. One day he said to me, *"Aunt Ruf living with this terminal illness is about to kill me"*. This let me know that he knew; my sister wanted to shield him from this knowledge.

As I visited every other day, Michael enjoyed hearing of my activities and writings. I read some of our family history to him. After we cleaned him up, he needed pain medicine, very expensive pain medicine, to help him rest. His insurance no longer paid. He was called back to work at the railroad after a hiatus of twelve years. Michael doesn't want to spend the two hundred ($200) for the medicine. He likes the sense of security from holding money. This gives me an opportunity to discuss values, materials and the hereafter. We must place our trust in God, not worry over material things or money. We will leave it here. Get right with God and have peace, to accept our situation.

It was hard to watch my 6'4" handsome nephew, fade before my eyes: thin with bones showing, hollow eyed, with a pain pinched face, a large ulcer on his behind, legs dangling with severe pain. Many days he was unable to eat, nauseated and vomiting large chunks of blood. Through it all saying, *"I'm all right, Aunt Ruf."* He was trying to eat a little of Me'Dear's and Mama Clara's cooking; he knows his grandmothers who were 86 (eighty six) and 80 (eighty) years old show their love through home cooked food. Although he keeps saying don't do this, they keep cooking. He says, *"You can't tell these old women what to do"*.

Michael's son, Michael Jr. will graduate from high school on June 15th, in Stone Mountain, Georgia. Demetria is now a 14 (fourteen) year old, six feet with a beautiful smile, braces off and she lost that baby fat. I see the pride in Michaels' face as he looked at his children. He talks to them about dating, marriage and school. Since his illness they come up every other week. During spring break, they stayed in Memphis. Michael Jr. was a great help in turning and getting Michael out of bed into a chair. At first I was concerned about them traveling in Michael Jr.'s old beat-up car, but I know God protects and is on the highway with them.

Michael Jr. wants to know if the family is being punished. I explain that all people suffer. *"We are not alone, many have the same problems, some worse than others. Yes, Aunt Janell, died last year from cancer and your grandfather, Emmett, Jr., died five months ago from cancer, and your great grandfather, Emmett, Sr., died last month of cancer"*. This shows a pattern in our families. So, we must concern ourselves with our lifestyles, and what we eat, drink, smoke and sexual activities.

LONNIE MAE

In Remembrance
July 1933-February 1994

L   *is for her laughter and love of life she was*

O   *one of a kind—who met everyone as a*

N   *neighbor for she never met a stranger. She*

N   *nurtured us all—husband, children, family and friends her*

I   *initiative kept the family gatherings going.*

E   *energetic*

M   *mother of seven children and was*

A   *active in church and community, She had*

E   *elasticity—the ability to bounce back due to her*

A   *attitude which was always positive, shown by her*

R   *radiant smile and we remember her*

C   *compassionate manner*

H   *hats, hair, hospitality, and her*

I   *involvement in Progressive Baptist Church and her*

E   *enthusiastic and effervescent (bubbling) life.*

PAMELA

P   MY PRETTY NIECE

A   ACTIVE

M   MAGNETIC

E   ENTHUSIASTIC

L   LOVING

A   ABLE

Pamela Ann was born—our only niece—what a pretty baby, and so loved by all the family, the Jones and the Pollards; Churches, Mt. Moriah Baptist Church and Mt. Pisgah CME and the beltline community, and all of Orange Mound. Naturally, she grew-up outgoing, kind and loving. She loved to dance, and never met a stranger. She loved her school, Melrose and the Tiger Football Team. She attended Lincoln University in Missouri. Her magnetic personality drew many to her. She was a member of a praise dance group at Mt. Moriah.

GREETINGS

Good morning. How are you? These are our typical greetings. This tells something of our culture. In America, health is an important concern. Are you well, mentally, physically and spiritually?

I read in the paper of another shake-up in the Department of Mental Health. I remember when patients were removed from mental institutions during the 70's and the problems that followed: homelessness, care givers out for the money, crime and increased hospitalizations. We ask or talk about our mental wellness, but I wonder if we are truly concerned. From the government officials to individuals, we ask the question, but don't wait on the answer. Mentally, we are not well. Many of our relationships with one another are kept secret.

When we are asked, *"How are you?"* we don't tell of the sexual, child and physical abuse or the violence in many of our homes. Many times we have no stable home life. Today, my heart is heavy laden, for I think my son took $20.00 from my wallet. He denied this but, he is not a responsible person; he has trouble keeping a job and has no direction or goals in life. My heart is broken, for I feel we are responsible for his lack of direction. I went back to work fulltime, when he was two years old and we moved from Cloverdale at the same time; we no longer had stable and dependable babysitters. I wondered if one of them might have been dealing in prostitution, for I suspected her boyfriend was a pimp. Bill and I were so busy with our professions and church work.

So, I don't tell people of my mental health. Many times when they ask, they don't wait on an answer anyway. Our relationships are part of our problems. With all types of communications; phones in cars, beepers and computers—we are still a lonely society. With the media portraying a fun loving happy society, many of us are depressed because we don't have this type of life. Since I have lost trust in my son, I am miserable. Questions are always present, is this real or a lie. I, who was always positive, now look at all relationships with suspicion. How many people have lost their sense of trust in relationships with mankind and government?

PEACE

Monday, February 21, 1966, I arrived in Dallas at 10:10 A.M. It was a dreary and cloudy day. How different the flight and the weather of seven years ago. I was flying in for the birth of Gregory Theodore Walter, Jr., My first grandchild. O, the joy—sun shining, bright day. There were big smiles on our faces: father, mother, and grandmother. Today, tears won't stop flowing. I think maybe it's my allergy, but I know it's the death of my daughter's marriage. The pain of it all—three little boys, the youngest six months old, the loss of their suburban home, the fellowship and friends of the Pleasant Grove Baptist Church family and the relationship with her in-laws.

My mind goes back to my parents' divorce and the bitter, hostile feelings. My father was awarded custody of the two girls. Mother was paid off with a measly thousand dollars ($1,000). Returning us to her after a few months when he was ready to remarry, and his new wife would have no place for his children. There, the hurt of a thirteen (13) year old, trying to hide the fear, especially from my sister.

So, I sit in the Airport of Dallas… But as I look back, I realize God was there, guiding me through and I look back and say: *"It was for my good".* For it made mother a stronger woman, no more fights or bitter hostile words; peace; no money, but determination. Love of family… Peace… Pass it on.

CANCER

Even though this summer has been a trying time for me; Linda's divorce, the absence of her children at our 4th of July celebration and Emmett's illness, I still hear 'I'm blessed'. There's joy in my soul. For in the midst of all the suffering and illnesses, we have a comforter, the Holy Spirit, who lets me know *"you are not alone"*. Whatever the trial, *I am with you*, says our God. This consolation and the knowledge he has never failed me, for great is his faithfulness, is my assurance.

I'm pondering over the anxiety and fear we have of the word cancer. In the last month, three people close to me have experienced hearing the dreaded word as a diagnosis. God tells me:

C   call upon God for strength to endure for He

A   answers prayer… My prayer is not necessarily to make us well… but make us whole in the sense of knowing him and realizing only relationships matter. Ask him to

N   navigate, guide and direct us, the relatives and friends. He knows our fear. Let us use fear as a motivator. Use our time wisely…loving, caring, showing concern for others. It's alright to

C   cry in our pain…but the comforter is there, let us experience and show many instances of compassion and concern, as we

E   express our love for one another and to God who is our

R   refuge…the safe place we have been seeking.

WEEPY EYES

There's a pool of water under my left eye,
It contains the sorrows of years gone by; disappointments, disillusions and distress.
Of husband, children and broken relationships
Of the unemployed and working poor,
Children and seniors going to bed hungry,
Young men standing on street corners or languishing in jail.
This pool at times over flows, this pool of water
Under my left eye.
A river flows from my right eye
A steady stream of joy and peace that only God can bring.
Marriage, birth of children, grandchildren,
Lasting childhood friendships.
Parents living into their late eighties
The joy of living
This river reminds me of God's love, guidance and direction.
These weepy eyes are full with
Sorrows and joy
As they flow down my face
And I cry for my race.
I wipe the tears away and
Thank God for my joys
That outnumber my sorrows.
This river flowing from my Right eye.

BAE'S REFLECTIONS

"You Can Tell the World"

Well you can tell the world about this
You can tell the nation about that
Tell'em what the master has done
Tell'em that the gospel has come
Tell'em that the victory's been won
He brought joy, joy, joy, joy, joy, joy, into my heart.

Well my Lord spoke, he spoke so well
Yes he did, yes he did
Talked about the flames that burn in hell
Yes he did, yes he did
Now my Lord spoke, he spoke so well
Yes he did, yes he did
Talked about the children of Israel
Yes he did, yes he did
He brought joy, joy, joy into my heart

Well my Lord spoke, he spoke to me
Yes he did, yes he did
Talkin' about a man from galilee
Yes he did, yes he did
My Lord spoke, he spoke to me
Yes he did, yes he did
Talkin' about a man from galilee
Yes he did, yes he did
He brought joy joy, joy into my heart

Well i don't know but I've been told
Yes he did, yes he did
Streets of heaven are paved with gold

Yes he did, yes he did
Now the Jordan river is chilly and wide
Yes he did, yes he did
I got a home on the other side
Yes he did, yes he did
He brought joy, joy, joy into my heart

ABOUT THE AUTHOR

Rutha Jenkins Jones is a writer who has written and recorded a collection of stories and reflections entitled Bae's reflections, Another curve and the Gathering Tree that are based on her lively experiences as an African American girl in the rural communities of Hernando, Mississippi; her mental and physical awakenings in life as a teenager and young adult in the 1940's and 1950's within the segregated areas of Memphis, Tennessee; and as an phenomenal adult and her extensive travels around the world, from Europe to the Holy land of Israel to the mother land of Africa and in the United States of America.

Rutha J. Jones is a retired public health nurse, and volunteered as the local coordinator health advocacy services for the American Association of Retired Persons (AARP). She has done presentations on health, health delivery systems, connections on living, medical and social security; in addition, she has volunteered with the Johnson Auxiliary to the Regional Medical Center at Memphis (The MED). Rutha also was active with Church Women United, a national ecumenical movement brings Protestant, Roman Catholic, Orthodox and other women of faith into one community of prayer, advocacy and service. She was Tennessee State President 2009–2011.

Rutha "Bae" Jones is a product of the Memphis city schools and a graduate of Hamilton High School. She is a proud graduate of freedmen's hospital school of nursing, Howard University in Washington, D.C. With continued study at the university of Tennessee, Southwestern (Rhodes) College and the University of Memphis. She was employed for 45 years at different medical facilities, with 25 (twenty-five) years at the Memphis Shelby

County Health Department and retired after 25 (twenty-five) years as the clinic supervisor of the sexually transmitted disease clinic.

Rutha Jenkins Jones, Elder, is currently a member at Liberation Community Presbyterian Church. She was a former member at Parkway Gardens Presbyterian Church for forty-five (45) years. She has served as chairperson of the board of Christian education, moderator of Presbyterian women of Parkway Gardens, and as the Sunday school teacher for pre-teens and church organist. On the Presbery level she served as a member of the coordinating team of Presbyterian women, congregational leadership and the committee on older adults.

Rutha Jones is the loving wife of Willie L. (Bill) Jones. They have been married for 69 years, and are the proud and dedicated parents of 3 (three) children, and the proud grandparents of 15 (fifteen) children and 19 (nineteen) greatgrandchildren. Rutha enjoys reading, writing, traveling, working in her church and keeping in contact with family and friends.

Sam Jenkins

SAM JENKINS (1855-1937)

Sam, my great grandfather, was born in 1855 in southern Mississippi. I was unable to find him in the census of 1870 in Mississippi. I wondered if Maybe He changed his name or came from a Louisiana plantation. Some of the big plantations of Warren County (Vicksburg) spilled over into Louisiana. I remember Aunt Inez mentioning Louisiana, but I can't remember the connection. I did find a Samuel Calvin Jenkins in the 1870 census living with messianic, presumably an eighty (80) year old grandmother in the Vicksburg area. He was the right age, fifteen; but was listed as deaf and dumb, unable to read or write. Sometimes he gave his parents birthplace as Alabama and at other times, the United States or unknown; or whatever he thought the questioner might want.

He was the last generation of slaves. He could be described as a tall black man with a crooked nose who lived with his family on the Ardmore plantation. His mother made many beautiful dresses for the ladies of the house. He played with the Ardmore children: Annie Elizabeth, Thomas and Henry. They played school where Annie Elizabeth taught him lessons her tutor had taught her. Sam listened well and soon was reading and writing. Henry teased him with knowledge he was sure Sam didn't know. Such as *"Sam doesn't know the earth is round"*. Sam marked these things as important and remembered them. He was unaware he talked like, had mannerisms, and a speech pattern of the Ardmores.

Mae Liza, his mother was a short, plump, dark skinned woman with typical Negroid features; thick lips, broad nose, and heavy hipped. She and her mother, a cook, came to Mississippi in the early 1800's. She was reared in and around the big house and had a sense of security although a slave. She sewed and helped in the kitchen. A quiet, stoic woman, who kept her anguish and frustration to herself when Samuel left; or as she thought, he was killed for his hot temper.

Sam's father, Samuel, it is thought, was brought to Mississippi in 1846 when more Negroes were needed to open up the lower southern states. He was considered temperamental or high strung and was sold frequently. He was a tall, dark man with a keen nose, thin lips and thick wooly hair. He was a loner, a man of few words, with a fiery temper who disappeared without revealing to Mae Liza or anyone, if it was planned.